understanding football

ISBN-13: 978-1-905540-07-5
ISBN-10: 1-905540-07-8

Author
Julia Hickey

Specialist Consultant
Simon Clifford

With thanks to Glyn Sutcliffe (indexer)

Throughout this publication, the use of pronouns he, she, him, her and so on are interchangeable and intended to be inclusive of both male and female footballers.

Published by

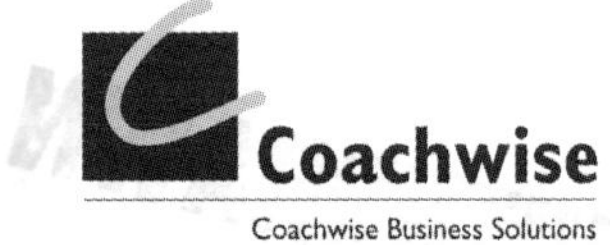

Coachwise Ltd
Chelsea Close
Off Amberley Road
Armley
Leeds LS12 4HP
Tel: 0113-231 1310 Fax: 0113-231 9606
Email: enquiries@coachwise.ltd.uk
Website: www.coachwise.ltd.uk

Produced and designed by Coachwise Business Solutions, a brand of Coachwise Ltd
If you wish to publish some material for your organisation, please contact us at
enquiries@coachwisesolutions.co.uk

If you are an author and wish to submit a manuscript for publication, please contact us at
enquiries@1st4sport.com

050300

Contents

Foreword

Football is the world's most popular game. It is played in every corner of the globe and many millions of people are involved as players, coaches, referees and spectators.

Understanding Football will benefit all those concerned with the game, offering valuable guidance on how to get started and the key issues within football – great for young, budding footballers and footballing adults alike. It will give these individuals a sound introduction to the game, providing them with the key information they need to get involved. It also cuts through the jargon surrounding the many laws and rules in football, which sometimes can be difficult to follow. By removing complications and offering an easy-to-follow breakdown of these laws and rules, *Understanding Football* not only improves understanding, but is also an extremely enjoyable read.

I have been inspired to assist with writing *Understanding Football* through my work with the Brazilian Soccer Schools. The incredible skills and flair of the great Brazilian teams and players excited me and made me want to learn more about football, from how they practised these skills through to the clubs that they played for. I have been lucky enough to meet many of these greats of the game and the one theme that each of them has highlighted is how important it is to become a good person and to learn the game well before you can think of becoming a good football player. This struck a chord with me and is what led me to help with the writing of this book. I hope that *Understanding Football* will aid and inspire young people to learn all that they can about the great game, including the intricacies of the laws and, perhaps most importantly, the true spirit in which the game should be played and followed.

Simon Clifford
(Owner and manager of Garforth Town Football Club
and founder of the Brazilian Soccer Schools)

Chapter 1

Getting the Most Out of *Understanding* ***Football***

There are three possible ways of reading this book. Whichever way you choose, have fun and enjoy football!

1 You can read the book from beginning to end.

Each chapter – from Chapter 5 onwards – is divided into three parts:

- The first part of the chapter provides information that will help you understand football, whether you want to watch or play the game.
- The second part is a **summary** of key information about the football laws dealt with in that chapter.
- The final part provides **training** tasks to help you check whether you have understood the rules and information covered in the chapter.

2 You can read just a chapter or a section of the book that you think might be useful to you.

- Scan through the book and look for the information (represented by icons) that interests you most. Here is a key to the icons.

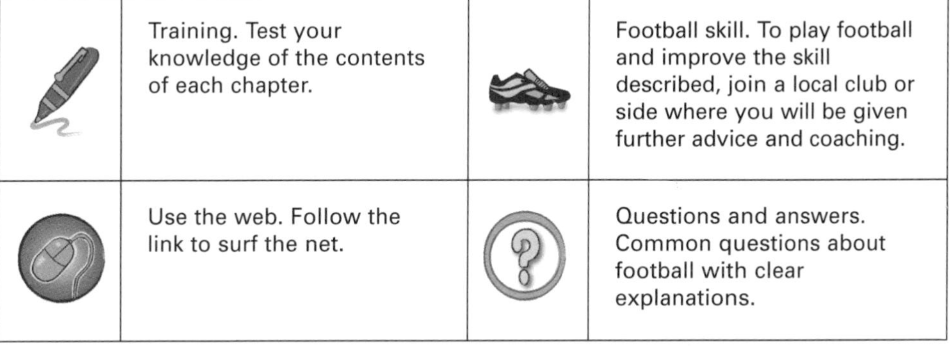

	Training. Test your knowledge of the contents of each chapter.		Football skill. To play football and improve the skill described, join a local club or side where you will be given further advice and coaching.
	Use the web. Follow the link to surf the net.		Questions and answers. Common questions about football with clear explanations.

- Use the summary sections of each chapter to brush up on your understanding.
- Test your understanding by completing the training activities at the end of each chapter.

3 You can complete the following quiz to find out what aspects of the game you need to sharpen up on. Check the answers to see how well you did and to identify the chapters you should work on.

Quiz

1 What is the Fair Play Code?

a A scheme that encourages school children to access professional football training. ☐

b A language used by football pundits. ☐

c A code that sums up what football ought to be about. ☐

2 How many substitutes are allowed in an official FIFA match?

a Three. ☐

b Six. ☐

c As many as the manager wants. ☐

3 How long is a football match, provided that it doesn't run into extra time?

a Half an hour. ☐

b An hour. ☐

c An hour and a half. ☐

4 What is an offside trap?

a It is a barrier to keep fans off the pitch. ☐

b It is a tactic sometimes used by defending players. The defenders move up the pitch, leaving the attackers nearer to their goal, so that the attackers are offside. ☐

c It is an electronic device used by assistant referees to check to see whether players have broken the offside rule. ☐

5 What will the referee do if a player commits the offence of deliberately handling the ball outside the penalty area?

a The referee will award the offending player's opponents an indirect free-kick. ☐

b The referee will award the offending player's opponents a throw-in. ☐

c The referee will award the offending player's opponents a direct free-kick. ☐

6 How far away from a kicker taking a direct free-kick must the defending players be?

a 10 yards. ☐

b 10 metres. ☐

c On the other side of the nearest boundary line. ☐

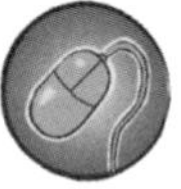

The referee's association has a monthly interactive quiz to test contestants' knowledge of the rules of the game and its history.
See how well you do at www.footballreferee.org

Quiz answers: 1, c (ch3); **2**, a (ch4 and ch5); **3**, c (ch5 and ch6); **4**, b (ch7); **5**, c (ch8); **6**, a (ch9).

Chapter 2

Football Through the Ages

This chapter explores how, over the centuries, football has become much more organised and how rules have developed in the interests of fair play.

Football in ancient times (2000 BC)

The Chinese played a football-like game called tsu chu (meaning 'to kick a stuffed ball of animal skin') while, in Japan, *kemi* involved kicking a ball through two bamboo shoots. The ancient Greeks played *episkyros* during the siege at Troy, while the Romans played *harpastum* and even had special buildings to practise in. It is possible that the Romans played this game in ancient Britain. None of these games are the same as football but they all have recognisable elements.

Football during the Dark Ages (AD 500–1066)

A game of football was said to have been played in Chester by two Saxon teams, using the head of a defeated Danish chief.

Football during the Middle Ages (1066–1485)

By this time, the ball was more likely to be an inflated pig's bladder than a human head! The teams were made up of large numbers of people, often apprentices.

There were very few rules and no referee, so these matches often turned into riots and irritated the authorities. Laws were passed to stop football in its tracks.

Key Dates in the Middle Ages

1314 The Lord Mayor of London banned football from being played inside the City walls.

1331 King Edward III passed laws against football being played.

An annual game, similar to medieval matches, is still played in Ashbourne in Derbyshire. The rules are simple: the game can't go on after nightfall, the ball is not to be transported by a vehicle and murder is forbidden.

Football in Tudor and Jacobean times (1485–1625)

Queen Elizabeth I and James I passed laws to try to put a stop to street football. Meanwhile, the nobility started to sponsor their own sides so that they could watch and bet on the outcome of a violent form of football called calicio. This game originated in Florence and records dating from 1530 mention a match held while the town was under siege.

Football in the 17th century

Oliver Cromwell is said to have been a keen football player in his youth. However, this didn't stop the Puritans from banning football along with Christmas, while closing theatres. Not surprisingly, these new laws didn't last long once the Puritans had been kicked out. They did succeed, though, in ensuring that no official football matches were played on Sundays until the 20th century.

Football in 18th and 19th centuries

At the beginning of this period, popular football continued much as before until some inspired teachers decided that football was just the thing to encourage team spirit, discipline and obedience in their pupils. Unfortunately, everyone made up their own rules so, when two teams from different places met, there was very little chance of a problem-free match. Sometimes, games were played according to one set of rules in the first half of the game and then another set in the second half.

Key Dates in the 18th and 19th Centuries

1862 Notts County, the oldest existing league club, was formed.

1863 Eleven clubs met in London to agree some rules. The Football Association (The FA) was formed and the first complete set of rules was decided upon.

1872 The first FA Cup competition was held. There were 13 matches. Corner kicks were also introduced into the rules to make the game fairer.

1885 Professionalism was permitted for the first time and so players were paid to play the game. This meant that football clubs needed to generate money to pay their professional players. Home and away fixtures were agreed as a way of increasing the number of football matches played.

1888 The English Football League was formed.

1891 The penalty kick rule was created as a result of a match between Stoke City and Notts County.

Key Dates in the 20th Century

1904 The Fédération Internationale de Football Association (FIFA) was formed.

1914 A Christmas game of football was played in no man's land by British and German soldiers during an informal truce between the warring troops.

1924 Away strips were worn by visiting teams for the first time. The rules were also changed to permit goals to be scored as a direct result of a corner kick.

1927 A match was broadcast on radio for the first time.

1976 Red and yellow cards were introduced as part of the referee's armoury.

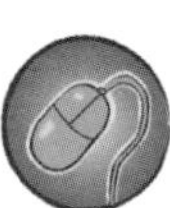

Find out more about football history by visiting http://www.fifa.com/en/history/index.html and www.scottishfa.co.uk and get interactive at www.nationalfootballmuseum.com

Chapter 3

Getting Started

An impromptu game of football can take place anywhere, whether it be in the street, park, beach or back garden. There's no need for goal posts; piles of bags or coats do the job just as well. There isn't even any need for a football; tennis balls, tin cans and scrunched-up balls of paper can all be used instead of a match ball. As for teams, you only require a roughly equal number of players on each of the two sides. No wonder football is called the 'people's game'!

What sort of equipment do I need to buy if I want to start playing football?

If you want to start playing football regularly, you should buy a pair of football boots so that you can play on a field; a football to allow practise even when you're by yourself; and a pair of shin pads with football socks for when you play in a match. These things will equip you to play and practise football.

I want to play football. Do I need to eat a special diet and be very fit?

As well as natural skill and plenty of practise, players need to look after their health and fitness. First-class players need to have strength, flexibility, speed, agility, coordination and cardiovascular fitness (when the heart and blood vessels efficiently pump oxygen around the body.

Players make sure they are consuming foods that suit their needs. Without a balanced and nutritional diet, the most talented player in the world will under-perform.

All professional players have dietary guidelines that they need to stick to in order to keep up their high-level performances. If players consume the wrong food and drink alcohol on a regular basis, they will not be able to train as hard or play for as long. Think about it: in a match, players need to compete for at least 90 minutes. This means that they need lots of carbohydrates to provide them with enough energy. Players also need to take care of their muscles – there is always the risk of injury – so consuming plenty of protein is also important.

It is also important to drink lots of fluid. Remember: fluid is lost through sweating during matches and training sessions. If your mouth feels dry and you are feeling hot, the chances are that you are dehydrated and this will affect health and performance. Therefore, drinks – but not fizzy sugary fluids – should be consumed before, during and after a training session or a match.

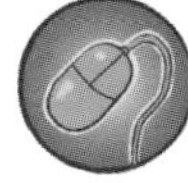

Find out about hydration by visiting http://news.bbc.co.uk/sport1/hi/health_and_ fitness/4289412.stm

It is also important that players avoid muscle injury. You should always warm-up, stretching your muscles and joints, before beginning a game. This helps you improve your flexibility and prevents you straining muscles. It is also important to cool-down after a game or a training session. Most of all, you need to know your own limits and not push yourself beyond them. If you do suffer an injury, it should be treated at once. Sports injuries can also be treated using a carefully adapted training regime that improves fitness gradually, over a period of time.

If you are just starting out on your playing career, it is important to eat sensibly. It would also be sensible to join a local club or team where you will receive coaching about playing skills, advice about what sort of exercise you should be doing and guidance about diet.

What sort of things do I need to know if I want to start playing or watching football?

You need to know the basics first: the pitch, the players, the length of a match, who the match officials are and the scoring system. These are all explained in The Laws of the Game (FIFA, 2005).

Remember that having the right attitude is just as important as having the correct equipment. And, of course, there have to be some rules and regulations for more organised matches.

The Fair Play Code

FIFA states that their Fair Play Campaign, which includes the Fair Play Code, was a partial result of the 1986 World Cup in Mexico and the behaviour of the England coach at the time, Sir Bobby Robson.

One of the two goals scored against England by Argentina was a result of a handball by Diego Maradona, who went on to describe it as 'the hand of God'. Rather than being angry and blaming the referee, Sir Bobby remained calm, despite the fact that this goal helped knock England out of the competition.

FIFA's 10-point code of conduct sums up what the 'beautiful game' should be about. Football, like any sport, should be played as fairly as possible – with the interests of everyone else involved in mind. Skill alone does not make a footballer great. Players, managers, coaches, officials and fans all need to have a good character and personality, and must think of others.

All players should:

- play fairly. There's no point in cheating – it's disrespectful to the opposing team, the player's own team and all the fans
- display mutual respect – no player wants to be treated in a derogatory way (as outlined in Chapter 8)

Player profile

© www.actionplus.co.uk

Sir Bobby Robson began his playing career as a winger for Fulham. He won 20 England caps between 1958 and 1962. He then went on to become the manager of Ipswich Town, overseeing a run of successful seasons before managing England in two nail-biting World Cups (1986 and 1990).

- understand and play by the rules of the game
- accept the referee's decision at all times
- be sporting in defeat.

The advice to amateurs and professionals, young and old, is straightforward: practise fair play and become a better player.

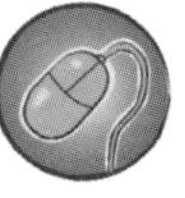

Find out more about the code and discover the ways in which football is changing the world by visiting http://www.fifa.com/en/fairplay

Summary

1 Football can be enjoyed at lots of different levels.

2 The equipment you need is minimal and doesn't have to be expensive.

3 A healthy diet is important, whether or not you play football. Try to eat five portions of fruit and vegetables a day. Avoid eating too much sweet or processed food as these foods tend to contain lots of refined sugars which are not as good for you

4 If you want to become an all-time great player, join a local team to get some more advice about diet and training

5 The laws and the Fair Play Code enshrine the spirit of football: equality between players and teams, safety and, of course, enjoyment for everybody involved in the game.

Chapter 4

All About the Basics

All about...the rules

- There are 17 rules or laws of football that have evolved since 1863 to ensure that the game is fair and exciting to play as well as to watch.
- The laws are the same whether players are amateur or professional.
- The laws can be adapted (if there is an agreement) to meet the needs of different groups of players, tournaments or competitions.

Whether you're playing a game of football or watching the match, you need to understand the information contained in these 17 laws.

Law 1 explains how big football pitches or a 'field of play' should be. It also explains the boundary lines and spots that are marked on the pitch, as well as all the other features a pitch needs before an organised match can be played.

Law 2 provides details about the football.

Law 3 explains how many players there should be on each team and how the substitution procedure works.

Law 4 explains what the players should wear.

Law 5 explains the role of the referee in ensuring that the laws of the game are abided by.

Law 6 explains what the two assistant referees do to help the referee ensure fair play during a football match.

Law 7 explains how many minutes there are in a match, how long the interval between the two halves of the match should be and how stoppage time is calculated.

Law 8 explains the procedure for starting a match. It also explains what a kick-off is and when it is used during a match.

Law 9 explains when a ball is 'in play' and when it is 'out of play'.

Law 10 explains the method of scoring. It also explains which team is the clear winner if both teams score the same number of goals (draw) in a match that requires there to be a winning team.

Law 11 explains what is meant by 'offside'. Chapter 7 explains the offside rule – a rule that is often open to disagreement. Players can be offside but not necessarily breaking the rules of the game.

Law 12 focuses on fouls and misconduct. It explains which offences are cautionable (yellow card offences) and which offences will result in a player being sent off the field of play (red card offences). It also explains when the referee will award opportunities, in the form of free-kicks or penalty kicks, to the team that has been fouled.

Law 13 explains what 'direct' and 'indirect free-kicks' are and the procedures involved in taking these kinds of set-pieces.

Law 14 explains what a 'penalty kick' is and the procedures for awarding and taking a penalty kick.

Law 15 explains how a 'throw-in' should be used to restart play and the correct procedure for taking a throw-in.

Law 16 explains 'goal kicks'.

Law 17 explains 'corner kicks'.

www.thefa.com/TheFA/RulesAndRegulations explains more about the laws and the decisions of football. The laws are made by the International Football Association Board. The board is responsible for ensuring that the rules retain their flexibility and enshrine fair play, so that the game is enjoyable to watch.

Also visit http://news.bbc.co.uk/sport1/hi/football/rules_and_equipment for more information.

All about...the different organisations involved with in football

These organisations are sometimes called governing bodies. They are responsible for regulating, promoting and organising tournaments. However, they all use the same set of football rules.

Table 1: The various football organisations

Organisation	Role	Website
The Football Association (The FA)	The governing body for football in England.	www.thefa.com
The FA Premier League	The administrative body for the top 20 clubs in the country.	www.premierleague.co.uk
The Fédération Internationale de Football Association (FIFA)	The governing body for world football.	www.fifa.com
The Football League	The administrative body of the Championship, League 1 and League 2.	www.football-league.co.uk
Union of European Football Associations (UEFA)	The governing body of European football.	www.uefa.com

All about...the football hierarchy

Clubs are organised into divisions/leagues. Each football season (the time when football is played each year), a certain number of teams are promoted up to the next league. Other teams are relegated into a lower division. Promotion and relegation is based on the number of points a team collects over the course of the season.

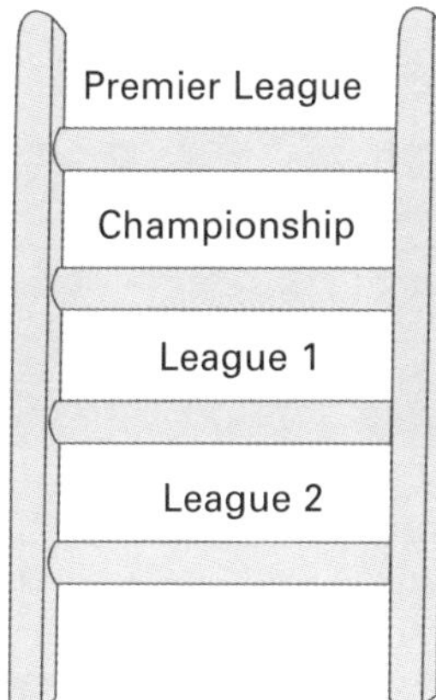

Figure 1: The football hierarchy

The best clubs in England are in the Premiership (this is another word that is used to describe the Premier League), which is the highest division in the country. Their stadiums must meet very high safety standards, well as being able to seat large numbers of fans. The second highest league is the Championship, followed by League 1 and then League 2. Each of these divisions/leagues are likely to have arranged a sponsorship deal so the name of the league will have the sponsor's name at the start of the title. For example, The Coca-Cola Championship (as shown in the picture above).

Some important competitions and trophies

The **FIFA World Cup**, played every four years, is the most prestigious football competition and its trophy is the most sought after. England won the World Cup in 1966.

Player profile

Sir Bobby Moore (1941–1993) Bobby played for Fulham and West Ham United as well as being a first-class defender for England on more than 100 occasions (90 of these were as captain). His career, spanning two decades, began at the age of 16 when he made his first appearance for West Ham Colts. He was named Footballer of the Year in 1964 before going on to captain England in their unforgettable 1966 World Cup campaign.

The **European Champions League** competition is a continental tournament. Places in the competition are determined by how well a club has done in its home country. This is called the domestic league performance. By doing well in their domestic leagues, teams can win a place in the European Champions League. Once teams have qualified for the event proper (there are qualifying stages for teams that aren't awarded an automatic place), they are then put into a group of four teams, with the two top teams of each mini-league progressing to the knockout phases.

Liverpool celebrate winning the European Champions League in 2005

The **UEFA Cup** is aimed at teams who just missed out on qualifying for a place in the Champions League, or who qualified through a domestic cup competition. It is run in a similar way to the Champions League, as is the African Nations Cup, Asian Nations Cup, COPA America and the Oceania Cup.

Then there's **The FA Cup**, where all teams in England, from the Premier League to the Northern Counties East League, compete for the oldest domestic cup in the world. As there are so many teams involved, there has to be a well-organised system for whittling down the teams so that the final rounds of the cup don't last too long.

While professional teams are guaranteed a place in the cup, amateur teams play in preliminary rounds to progress to the next, qualifying round. These qualifying rounds are played on a regional basis and the winners of these qualifying rounds go on to play games with the professional clubs.

Next come the proper rounds of The FA Cup. There are six proper rounds, plus the quarter- and semi-finals and then the final itself. The Premier League teams enter the competition in the third round. Clubs are drawn against each other when their names are randomly drawn out of a hat in pairs. The resulting match is then played at the home ground of the team that is drawn first out of the hat. The winner of the game goes on to the next round. If both teams score the same number of goals (draw), a replay has to take place. If, in the replay, the teams can still not be separated, a penalty shootout will decide the outcome. Because of this, there can be shock results in The FA Cup. 'Giant killing', low-ranking teams can knock out prestigious clubs from the tournament – the results should never be taken for granted.

Find out more at www.theFA.com and at www.football-league.premiumtv.co.uk/page/Home

All about...famous stadiums

France has the **Stade de France**, just outside Paris; Mexico has the **Estadio Guillermo Canedo** that hosted two World Cup finals; Spain has the **Nou Camp**, home of Barcelona; and England has **Wembley Stadium**. However, the biggest stadium in world football is the **Maracaná** in Rio de Janeiro, Brazil. The stadium has an official capacity of 183,000 people, although it has been known to hold 200,000 spectators.

Why not take a virtual tour of the new Wembley Stadium by visiting www.wembleystadium.com

Two of England's most famous teams

The England team that won the World Cup in 1966 was managed by Sir Alf Ramsey. Three goals scored by Geoff Hurst ensured victory over West Germany.

The Manchester United team of 1999 won the English Premier League, The FA Cup and the Champions League, completing the Treble. The final of the latter competition was even more memorable as Manchester United, 1–0 down to Bayern Munich, scored two goals in the final two minutes to claim victory.

Manchester United celebrate their Champions League success in the Treble-winning season of 1999.

Chapter 5

The Ingredients of Football

This chapter is about the essential components that are required for an official football match. It also explores the way in which the game is controlled through the laws to ensure fair play.

All about...the field of play

The rules call the area where the game is played, 'the field of play'. This refers to the football pitch, its boundary lines, the goal posts and the corner flags.

The pitch

- Matches may be played on natural or artificial surfaces, though these are less common.

The best natural surface is well-drained turf. Games can be called off because of a waterlogged or frozen pitch.

Indoor matches are played on other man-made surfaces. The ball used and the footwear worn have to be suitable for these surfaces.

- The pitch must be rectangular.
- Football pitches must be a certain size, though this is fairly flexible!
- The length of the touchline must be greater than the length of the goal line.
- The pitch is marked with lines. These lines mark the boundaries of the pitch and show different areas of the field of play.
- None of the lines marking the boundaries of a football pitch should be more than 12 cm (5 ins) wide.
- Most line markings are white, though there is nothing in the rule-book mentioning a correct colour.

Boundary lines and different areas on the field of play

Each field of play should indicate:

- the **half-way line**. This does exactly what it says on the label and splits the pitch into two. Teams must be in their own half of the pitch when the game kicks-off or re-commences after a goal has been scored. Substitutes must come onto the pitch at the half-way line (there is more about this in Chapter 6)

Table 2: Range of permitted football pitch dimensions

	Metric	Imperial
Organised Matches		
Length (touchline)	90–120 m	100–130 yds
Width (goal line)	45–90 m	50–100 yds
International Matches		
Length (touchline)	100–110 m	110–120 yds
Width (goal line)	64–75 m	70–80 yds

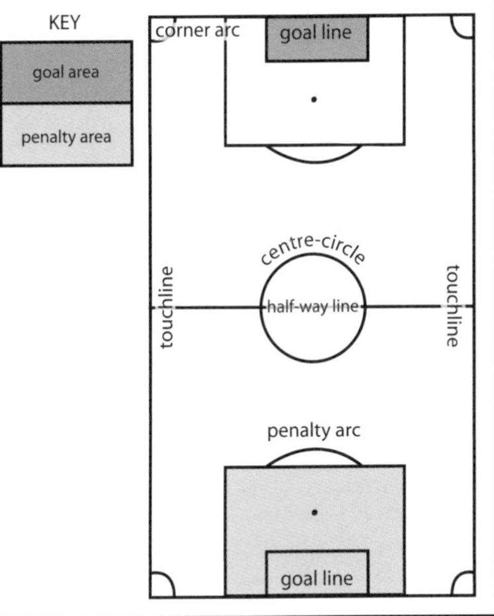

Figure 2: The field of play

- the **centre circle**. A centre mark indicates the midpoint of the half-way line. It is 9.3 m (20 yds) in diameter. This is used for kick-offs (there is more about this in Chapter 6)
- **four corner arcs**. These are quarter circles with a radius of 1 m (1 yd) drawn inside the field of play around each corner flag post. These boundaries are important for corner kicks (there is more about corner kicks in Chapter 9)
- **two goal areas**. Each marked goal area is a rectangle that is 5.5 m (6 yds) wide. They extend 6 yds from each goal post along the goal line and 6 yds into the playing area from the goal line. The goal area is also referred to as 'the 6 yd area'. When a goal kick is awarded to the defending team, to restart the game, the ball must be placed inside the goal area.
- **two penalty areas**. Each penalty area begins 16.5 m (18 yds) away from each goalpost. The width of the penalty area is 16.5 m (18 yds). The penalty area is also referred to as 'the 18 yd area' or 'the penalty box'. Only the goalkeeper is allowed in this area when a player from the opposing team takes a penalty kick (there is more about this in Chapters 6 and 9)
- **a penalty spot**, which is placed 11 m (12 yds) from the midpoint between the goalposts. There are two penalty marks on the pitch, one in each penalty area. This is the spot where players take penalty kicks awarded in the penalty area or in a penalty shoot-out (more about this in Chapters 6 and 9).
- **two penalty arcs**. An arc of a circle, with a radius of 9.15 m (10 yds) from each penalty mark, is drawn outside each penalty area. When a penalty is taken, players must not step inside the arc.

All about...flag posts

- To be no less than 1.5 m (5 ft) high.
- To have a non-pointed top for safety.
- To be placed vertically in each corner arc

There must be a corner flag in each of the four corners of the pitch.

All about...the goal

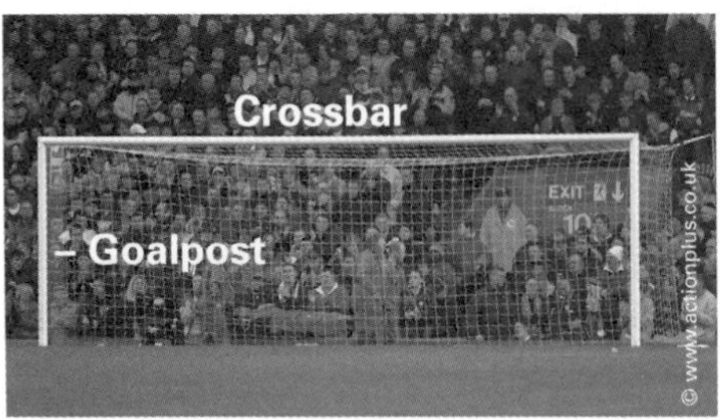

- The distance from the crossbar to the ground is 2.44 m (8 ft).
- The distance between the posts is 7.32 m (8 yds).
- Goalposts and crossbars must be white.
- The crossbar must be solid – rope can't be used.
- Goals (meaning the goalmouth) must be placed centrally along the goal line.
- Each goal post must be the same distance from the corner flag post nearest to it.
- The goalposts and the crossbar should be the same width and depth, which mustn't exceed 12 cm (5 ins). The goal lines should be the same width as the goalposts and the crossbar. This means the goal is a clear target and there is less chance of making a mistake about whether a goal has been scored or not.
- Nets may be attached to the goals and the ground behind the goal. Be careful that they are properly secured.

All about...the ball

The ball must be:

- spherical
- made of leather or another suitable material
- checked by the referee before the start of a game to make sure it meets the official standards.

Air pressure in the ball: This should be between 0.6–1.1 atmospheres.
Weight: This should be between 410 g and 450 g (14–16 oz)
Circumference: This should be between 68–70 cm (27–28 ins)

There are five different sizes of football available. A match-size ball is size 5.

Who provides the ball?
The home team usually provide the football.

Top tip: If you want to practise footwork and control, choose a size 2 Fotebol de salao football. It's smaller and heavier, which makes it an ideal combination for practising those all-important skills.

Want to bend it like Beckham? Master the **banana kick.**

Skill is required, but the right ball helps. The fewer panels there are on a ball the less stable it is, so the more it can be curved.

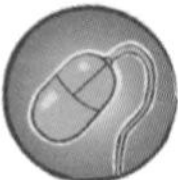

Find out how to curl a ball at www.bbc.co.uk/science/hottopics/football

All about...caring for a football

- Apply the 'thumb test' to check that the ball isn't over- or under-inflated – there should be some give, but not much.
- Don't over inflate the ball – it is more likely to crack or burst.

- After using the ball, wipe the mud off with a damp cloth.
- Let the ball dry naturally if it is wet. Putting a leather ball near a heater will cause it to crack.
- If you are storing the ball for some time, partly deflate it.

All about...the players

- A match is played by two teams.
- There are 11 players on each team, including the goalkeeper.
- A referee will not start a game if a team tries to start a match with fewer than 11 players.
- Most matches played allow a maximum of three substitutions, although non-competitive games, such as pre-season friendlies, may allow more. A substitution is when one player comes off the pitch and is replaced by another player from the same team.

The names of the substitutes must be given to the referee before the match. Substitutes who have not been registered before the start of play are not allowed to take part in that game.

If the referee sends someone off the pitch, can a substitute take the other player's place?

No! If a player has been sent off, the team cannot bring another player on. The team has to continue the match a player down.

What happens if the referee sends a goalkeeper off?

If a goalkeeper leaves the pitch, any one of the remaining players may be substituted for a goalkeeper, or an outfield player may become a makeshift goalkeeper.

Table 3: The number of substitutes permitted for different competitions and tournaments

Type of match	Number of substitutes allowed
An official match	• Three. • Priot to the match, teams have to nominate three to seven players who may be selected as substitutes.
All other matches	• As many substitutes as the two teams want, so long as the number is agreed before the match and the referee is informed. • Otherwise, no more than six.

Substitutes coming onto the pitch without the referee's permission will be cautioned.

Can a player come back on the pitch once they've been substituted for someone else?

Once a player has been taken off the field and replaced, they are not allowed back on.

All about...the goalkeeper

- Each goalkeeper wears a kit that is different from the other players, the referee and the assistant referees.
- Goalkeepers are allowed to wear goalkeeper's gloves and tracksuit bottoms.
- Goalkeepers usually defend the goal area and the goal, but they can go anywhere on the pitch. The goalkeeper Jimmy Glass once scored for Carlisle United in the final minutes of a game to save the team from relegation.
- The goalkeeper is the only person who is allowed to handle the ball in the penalty area.

Did you know?

England played in 10 World Cup final tournaments during the 20th century.

The goalkeepers in the squads were:

- Bert Williams (1950)
- Gilbert Merrick (1954)
- Colin MacDonald (1958)
- Ronald Springett (1962)
- Gordon Banks (1966 and 1970)
- Peter Bonetti (1970)
- Peter Shilton (1982,1986 and 1990)
- David Seaman (1990 and 1998)

All about...the players' kit

Players must not wear anything that is dangerous to themselves or to other players, such as jewellery.

Every player on the team (excluding the goalkeeper, who should wear a distinctive top) wears an identical strip to show which team they belong to. The captain of each team is identified by an armband tied around their arm.

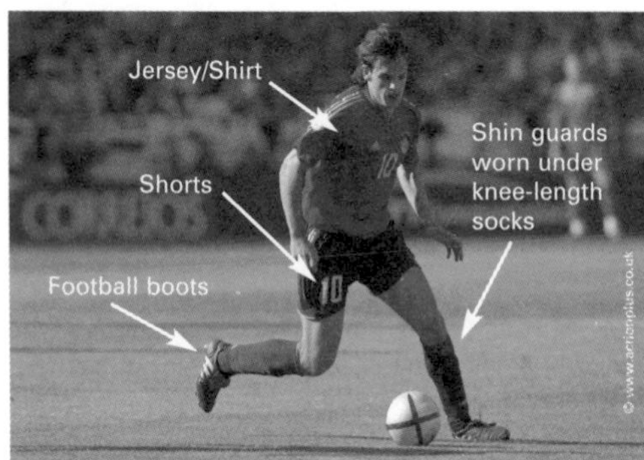

Players sent from the pitch for being improperly dressed will be cautioned if they return to the pitch without the referee's permission.

When two teams with similar coloured strips play each other, the visiting team will wear a different strip. This is called an away strip.

National teams wear strips with logos that are representative of the country to which they belong.

Choosing a pair of football boots

Remember, you will need different footwear if you're playing indoors.

Personal choice has a lot to do with choosing a pair of football boots. Some players, such as Thierry Henry, favour light boots as they can help with acceleration. Others, like Roy Keane, favour more traditional football boots. The main thing to ensure when buying boots is comfort. The external appearance may be appealing but if the boot is uncomfortable, you won't be at the top of your game. There is also a range of soles available, moving from the traditional screw-in studs to moulded blades. Some players favour blades, as research suggests that they help with turning and acceleration. Others prefer the grip that the conventional metal stud offers.

All about...the referee

The referee makes sure the football rules are followed during the match.

Referees have the authority to take disciplinary action, against both players and managers/coaches from the moment they come onto the pitch until they leave, after the final whistle.

The referee:

- usually wears a black/yellow strip – so as to stand out from the two teams
- checks the ball before the start of a match
- tosses a coin before the match to decide who gets the kick-off and which end a side will be playing from (there is more about this in Chapter 6)
- works with two assistant referees and a fourth official in professional matches
- acts as timekeeper for the match
- stops, pauses or ends the match if any rules are broken or someone from outside the game interferes with the match
- starts the match and restarts play if it has been stopped to deal with problems (this is usually done by blowing a whistle)
- controls who comes on and off the field, whether they are injured, have been substituted for another player or have been disciplined for breaking the rules
- takes disciplinary action against players guilty of breaking the rules. The players and the fans can see how the referee is penalising a guilty player because the referee will hold a yellow card up to signify a caution and a red card to signify that a player is being sent off
- takes action against team officials who fail to behave responsibly
- writes a report at the end of a match.

Signals

Communicating between officials and with the two teams is an essential part of being a good referee. The assistant referees (formerly known as linesmen) use flags to communicate with the referee on the pitch. Players and fans can also interpret these signals. The use of flags helps to make the events on the pitch easier to understand.

The referee uses a whistle, two cards (yellow and red) and a number of hand signals to direct and inform players. He will also speak to the players. There are a number of signals illustrated throughout *Understanding Football* for you to keep an eye out for.

Why do some referees wear two watches?

One watch keeps the time of the match – 45 minutes for each half (90 minutes in total). The referee will use the other watch to note the minutes and seconds of stoppage time (time when the referee stops the game to deal with problems, such as injured players). These extra minutes are added to the total time so that the game can continue for the right time period after the original 90 minutes are over.

Who is the best referee of all time?

Jose Mourinho, the Chelsea boss, described Italian **Pierluigi Collina** as the 'world's best referee'.

Referee profile

Pierluigi Collina, Italy's formidable and world-renowned referee, began his career in 1977. By 1995, he was on FIFA's list of referees and in 1996, he demonstrated his skilful interpretation of the football laws during the Olympic Games. Little wonder, then, that this tough but fair ref went on to referee the 2002 World Cup final between Brazil and Germany.

All about...assistant referees

- There are two assistant referees.
- They indicate whether a ball has gone out of play.
- They tell the referee which side is entitled to a corner kick, goal kick or throw-in.
- They can tell the referee if a player is in an offside position.
- During a penalty kick, they look to see whether the goalkeeper moves forward before the ball has been kicked.
- During a penalty kick, the assistant referees look to see whether the ball has crossed the line.
- They assist to ensure that the substitution process flows smoothly.
- The assistant referees use flags to signal events during the match.

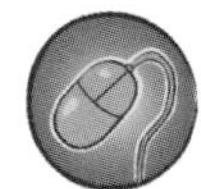

Find out more about Collina at http://www.pierluigicollina.it/

Who is the fourth official and what does she do?

The fourth official is a substitute for the referee and her assistants. If a referee is injured or ill, the fourth official can step in to take her place. The fourth official makes sure that everything runs smoothly off the pitch; she checks that the substitution procedure is followed correctly and confirms that the substitutes are wearing the correct equipment. She also ensures that the coaching and managerial staff stay clear of the pitch and abide by the laws of the game. If a replacement football is required, the fourth official provides the ball and she will also help write the match report.

All about...the length of a match

- A football match is 90 minutes long.
- The match is divided into two halves of 45 minutes each.
- There is a half-time interval of approximately 15 minutes.
- Matches can last longer than 90 minutes because of allowances made for time lost during the game. This used to be called injury time but is now referred to as 'stoppage time'.
- Stoppage time can be added to a match by the referee (who keeps a record of minutes lost) to make up time lost because of substitution(s), dealing with injured players, taking injured players off the pitch or players wasting time.
- Some matches require an outright winner. One of the ways of drawing the game to this conclusion is to play extra time. This usually consists of playing for an extra 30 minutes, split into two halves with the teams playing 15 minutes each way.
- If there is still no winner after extra time, the match is decided by penalties.

What happens if a match is abandoned?

Usually, the match is replayed at another time, unless the competition rules say otherwise.

All about...winning

The aim of the game is to win! Teams win by scoring more goals than their opponents within the time allowed.

A goal is scored when the ball passes completely over the goal line, between the goalposts and under the crossbar.

Each team uses attackers to move the ball forward, towards the goal where the opposing goalkeeper is standing. Defenders try to stop goals being scored.

A coin is tossed to decide which team chooses the goal they want to aim for. After the first half, the teams swap ends; this means that the two teams have an equal opportunity to score goals at either end of the pitch. This prevents one team having an advantage or disadvantage, caused by factors such as wind or glare from the sun. At the end of the match, the team with the most goals wins. If both teams have an equal score, it is called a draw.

What happens if a defender accidentally knocks the ball into the goal he is trying to protect?

The player scores a goal for the opposition – an own goal.

Summary

1 There are 17 rules. These rules are flexible so that they can be changed to meet the needs of different players and competitions.

2 Extra time can be played in cup matches if the teams are still level after 90 minutes.

3 The team that scores the most goals wins the match. If neither side scores or if they both score the same number of goals, it is called a draw.

Training

A Here is a partially completed plan of a football pitch.

i Label all the different areas and boundary lines.

ii Add in the corner arcs and the penalty arcs.

iii Add the dimensions of a pitch of international standard.

B Watch a football match. Identify the different features on the field of play.

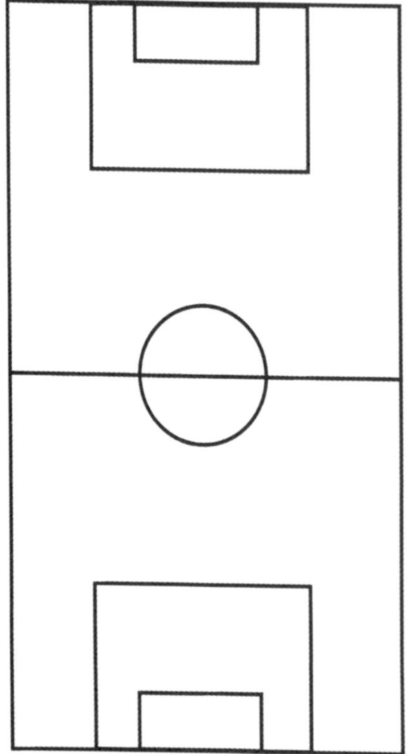

C Watch a football match. Note down the ways in which the referee and assistant referees control the match.

D There should be nine items in the referee's kitbag, but three are missing. What are they?

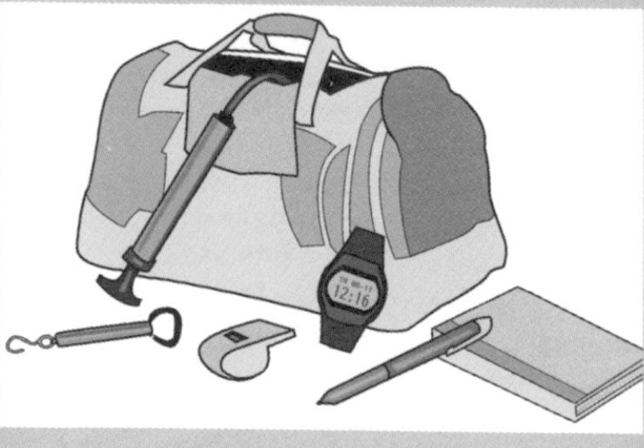

E Health and safety is an important part of any football match. List the ways Law 1 and Law 4 protect the players from injury.

Chapter 6

Following the Progress of a Match

Starting a match

The two teams line up on the half-way line with the two team captains facing one another.

The referee tosses a coin.

The team that loses the toss wait to see what the other captain's choice is.

The team that wins the toss decides which goal it will attack in the first half of the match. In the second half of the match, the teams change ends. The team that loses the toss will kick off.

The players take their place on the pitch:

- All players must stand in their own half of the pitch at the start of the game (and for the start of the second half).
- At the start of the match, the only people allowed in the centre circle are members of the team taking the kick-off.
- The opponents of the team taking the kick-off must be at least 9.15 m (10 yds) from the ball until it is in play.

The referee places the ball on the centre spot in the centre circle. It should be stationary. This is repeated at the start of the second half of the game.

To start the match, the referee blows a whistle and raises her arms so that they are outstretched and parallel at shoulder level. If the referee needs to restart the match following a temporary stoppage that is not covered by the laws, she will often use the dropped ball technique.

Three points to note:

- The ball is in play when it is kicked and moves forward from the spot where the referee placed it before the start of the match.
- The kicker is not allowed to touch the ball again until it has been touched by another player.
- A goal cannot be scored until a second player has touched the ball – a goal can only be scored from kick-off if it has been passed to a second player or the goalkeeper touches it before the ball goes into the net.

What is a 'dropped ball'?

A dropped ball is a way of restarting a match after a temporary stoppage. The referee drops the ball to the ground at the spot where the match was stopped. The ball is in play as soon as the ball touches the ground.

It is used where there is no other prescribed method of restarting a game. This process may take place more than once before a game is successfully restarted. If a player touches the ball before it reaches the ground, the referee will drop the ball again. In addition, if the ball leaves the field of play before a player has touched it, the referee will drop the ball for a second time.

Player positions and strategy during a match

A team can be divided into three main groups:

Defenders The players closest to the team's own goal.

Midfielders The players in the middle of the pitch.

Strikers The players closest to the opponents' goal, leading the attack.

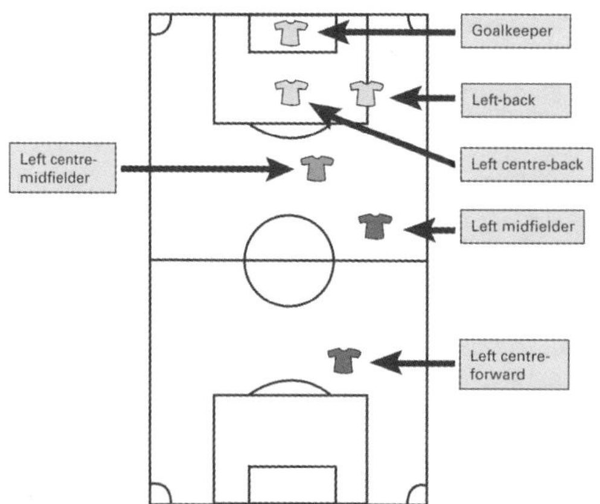

Figure 3: The positions of the players on the pitch

The positions are identified as left or right, based on the direction that the goalkeeper is looking when he stands in his goal facing the pitch.

Attacking and defending

The team that has possession of the ball tries to move it into the opposing team's half of the pitch to try and score a goal. The team without the ball try to defend their goal from the attackers and to gain possession of the ball from the other team so that they can then attack.

In order to attack or defend successfully, players must work as a team. When a team loses possession of the ball, all the players must defend, trying to win the ball back.

Formations

As the game of football developed, teams tried different formations to get the most out of each player. Formations depend on the team's style of play. If a team is trying to score a goal in the last few minutes, the manager may choose to use three or more strikers whereas, if the team is playing defensively, the manager may only choose one striker and have five defenders.

The 4–4–2 formation

The 4–4–2 formation is one most commonly used by English teams because it creates a balance between defence and attack. The number of players in defence and midfield mean the strikers can almost entirely concentrate on scoring goals.

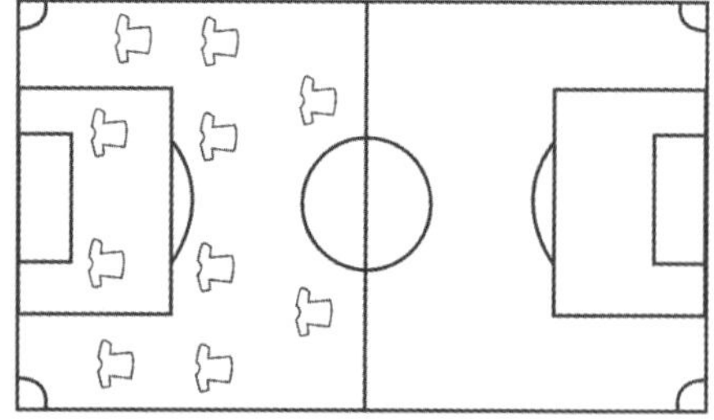

Figure 4: The 4–4–2 formation

The 5–3–2 formation

Although this formation seems more defensive, it allows for the wingbacks, to run up and down the wings, so that they can produce crosses into the opposition's penalty area, as well as defend their own area when necessary. This formation creates strength down the centre of the team because there are always three defending players in place.

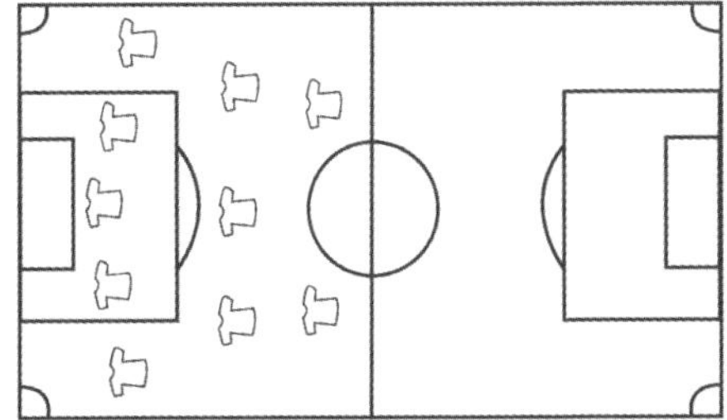

Figure 5: The 5–3–2 formation

Using a sweeper

This system is much more defensive. The sweeper – the lone player behind the rest of the defence – can move around the pitch behind the four defenders, stopping any attackers who get through the defensive formation.

Changing formation

The formation a team adopts is changed by the manager for a number of reasons. If the team is winning the game, the manager may decide to substitute one of the attackers for a defender to add some strength at the back. Similarly, if the team is losing, an extra striker or midfielder might be brought on to improve the team's chances of scoring. The captain or substitute entering the match can let their teammates know what the changes are.

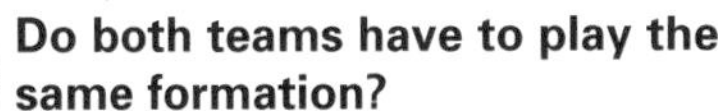

Do both teams have to play the same formation?

No, although managers try to guess what formation their opponent will adopt to cancel their players out or to counter it.

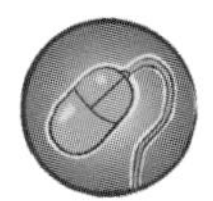

Find out more about formations at http://news.bbc.co.uk/sport1/hi/football/rules_and_equipment/default.stm

Attacking roles and skills

Part of the skill of the attacker is being in the right place at the right time. The team moves the ball up the pitch towards the goal, trying to create a chance for the strikers to score a goal.

- This means attackers need to anticipate where the ball is going to be.
- They also need to be able to outwit the defenders so that they can escape the players who are marking them. They need to create space.

Strikers

Strikers are football players who have a talent for scoring goals – they are good 'finishers' (this means that once the ball has been set up by the other players, they are able to score past the opposing goalkeeper).

Sir Bobby Charlton notched up 49 international strikes for England and Michael Owen confirmed his place in the ranks of England's notable strikers when he scored a hat-trick against Germany in Munich in 2001. Strikers have a talent for shooting and may also be good in the air – this means that they are able to produce some excellent headers.

Player profile

Seemingly blessed with similar skills to Paul Gascoigne, **Wayne Rooney** epitomises the word 'genius'. With a capability of scoring goals from anywhere on the field, the England hotshot could well go on to set his own goalscoring records at international level, having opened his account aged just 17.

Scoring goals

In each game there may be very few chances to shoot at the goal, so it is important that the players seize on any opportunity. This means that players, most likely to be strikers, have to keep their cool under pressure, assess the distance to the goal and kick the ball with power and accuracy.

Shooting

- If you want the ball to stay low, lean over it as you strike it and hit the middle of the ball.
- If you want the ball to go high, lean back as you kick the ball, striking the bottom to create lift.

It would not be good if a striker lost his or her balance. Look closely at a striker in action. They often spread their arms to improve their balance.

Heading the ball into the goal

With power and accuracy you will be able to head a ball into the goal. A good header involves a strong jump so that the ball can be headed down towards the ground, rather than up. If the ball is moving on an upward trajectory, it will go over the cross bar. The forehead should be used to help create power and to avoid injury.

Defending roles and skills

It is up to the goalkeeper and the defenders to stop the opposing team from scoring a goal.

Heading the ball away from the goal

When defenders head the ball, they want the ball to travel as far as possible away from their end of the pitch, or into the possession of their team's attackers. This means that the ball has to travel further. The trajectory is different. Players need to head the ball from beneath so that it travels up into the air during its trajectory.

The goalkeeper

- The goalkeeper organises the defence and must shout clear instructions to the team's defending players.
- The goalkeeper can use any part of his/her body to stop the ball.

Player profile

Rio Ferdinand possesses all the credentials needed to continue to thrive in international football, having made his full debut for his country back in March 1998 against Switzerland. The central defender, a product of the West Ham United youth academy, is the envy of others with his calmness on the ball and brilliant skill and distribution.

- Goalkeepers need to be confident that they can catch and stop the ball.
- It is important for the goalkeeper to be positioned between the goal and the ball.

What does it mean when a goalkeeper 'narrows the angle'?

The goalkeeper sees an attacker coming straight towards the goal. The 'goalie' (another term for the goalkeeper) then moves towards the ball, giving the attacker less of a goal to aim at. This needs to be done carefully because there is a risk of leaving the goal open to the attacker.

Top tip: To stop a high ball, form a 'W' shape with both hands – the thumbs should almost touch (as shown below). Spread all the fingers and bend your forearms to absorb the power of the ball.

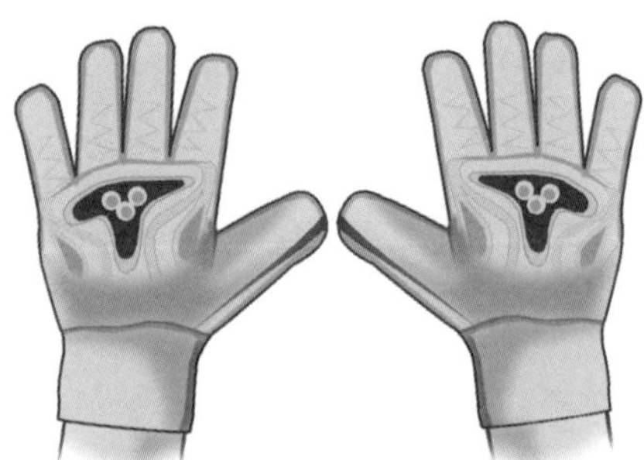

Figure 6: The goalkeeper's 'W'

Player profile

David Seaman. Standing 6ft 3ins this Rotherham born goalie has much more than height amongst his credientials as an experienced goalkeeper. With more that 1000 career games during his time playing for Leeds, Peterborough, Queens Park Rangers, Arsenal and Manchester City he has notched up so many saves that he has been nick-named 'safe hands'. His skills as a goal keeper made him a respected member of the England squad on many occasions.

© www.actionplus.co.uk

Other defenders

The rest of the **defenders** on a team try to stop opposing attackers from gaining possession of the ball. They do this by **marking** a player. This means that they stop their opponent passing, shooting or receiving the ball. Defenders need to be aware of attackers using the **blind side** (the area the defender marking the attacker has difficulty covering). This is the place that the attacker will try to be in when the ball is passed. Ideally, defenders try to **close-down** the attackers by marking them so closely that the attackers have limited opportunity to receive or play the ball.

Defenders need to stay between attackers and the goal, and they need to dispossess the ball from their opponent fairly. To do this, they need to be able to tackle their opponent. It is important that the tackle is legal. This means that the rules recognise that it is a fair method of removing the ball from an opposing player. If a player tackles another player using a method that the rulebook doesn't permit, it is called a foul.

 **A block tackle**

This tackle is used to stop an opponent shooting or passing. The defender will move towards the player with the ball and stretch out her leg to get the foot as close to the ball as possible (as shown in the picture below). The closer she gets, the more likely it is that she will succeed in blocking the attacker's pass or shot.

If possible, wait for one of the following situations before making a challenge:

- The attacker losing balance.
- The attacker losing control of the ball.
- The attacker losing at the ball.

© www.actionplus.co.uk

 **A sliding tackle**

This is a dramatic-looking tackle that defenders use when they feel the attacker is getting too close to the goal. It should not be attempted before the block tackle has been mastered.

To perform this tackle, come alongside your opponent before making the challenge. Try to tackle from the side and across the path of the attacker – the player must have the ball or the tackle becomes a foul!

Remember: Your foot must be at the side of your opponent before you make the tackle, or the referee will see it as a tackle from behind, which is not allowed.

- The key point to remember is that the ball has to be taken first, not the player.
- Use the leg furthest away from your opponent. Pass the ball away from the attacker as you slide in front of the player.
- Get up quickly!

There is always a risk that the slide tackle will result in a foul or that the defender will miss-time it and leave the rest of the defence exposed.

Follow the link to slide away at

© www.actionplus.co.uk

http://news.bbc.co.uk/sport1/hi/football/skills and see an animated explanation of the sliding tackle.

Midfield roles and skills

Midfield players need to be versatile. They must help with defence or attack, wherever they are needed most. Midfielders are often picked to be team captain because they have an overview of what is happening on the pitch. They are also best placed to bring about a change of formation, if circumstances require it.

Ball control is also an essential skill for a midfield player.

Kicks and passes used during matches

Back passes

Instead of advancing the ball up the pitch, a player passes the ball back down the pitch towards their own goal to a teammate to keep the ball safe (as pictured below).

© www.actionplus.co.uk

Back heeling the ball

The player kicks the ball backwards with his heel. This can be a quick way of releasing the ball and one that the opponent might not expect to be used.

Cross

This pass crosses the pitch and is aimed towards the opponent's penalty area. It can create chances for the strikers.

© www.actionplus.co.uk

http://www.givemefootball.com/coaching/coach_crossing

Dribble

The player moves the ball forward using small touches, keeping control of it at all times to ensure that a defender can't tackle him.

Nutmeg

The ball is passed between the defender's legs by an attacker and then, having run around the defender, the attacker regains the ball.

Overhead kick

The player kicks the ball back, over their own head. In this case, the player stands with his/her back to the goal and takes a shot. If overhead kicks are used without care for nearby players, they could result in a caution or even being sent from the field of play.

The ball in play and the ball out of play

The two teams use strategy and skill to kick or pass the ball up and down the pitch, so long as the ball remains in play. The assistant referees are watching to see whether the ball remains in play or not. If the ball goes out of play, she will signal as shown on the left.

The ball is **out of play** in the following circumstances:

- If the ball has completely crossed the goal line or touchline. It doesn't matter whether the ball has rolled over the lines along the ground or sailed through the air above the lines, either way, the ball is out of play.
- If play has been stopped by the referee.

The ball is **in play** at all other times, including when it rebounds from a goalpost, crossbar, cornerflag post and referee, so long as it remains on the pitch.

Who decides if a ball is in or out of play?

Law 9 is very clear about the circumstances in which a ball is in or out of play. If the ball has clearly gone over the goal lines or the touchlines, or the match has been halted by the referee, there is no doubt. The referee, with the advice of the assistant referees, makes the final decision as to whether the ball is in play or not.

The best advice for a player is to play to the whistle.

What does it mean to 'play to the whistle'?

Although players, at times, may anticipate the referee's decision, sometimes the referee and his assistants may miss an event or interpret it differently. Either way, players that disagree with the decision should carry on playing rather than protesting – the referee's decision is final and he won't change his mind.

What happens if the ball bounces off the referee and goes straight into the goal? Is a goal scored?

If the ball deflects off the referee, the ball is still in play. This means that, yes, a goal is scored.

Why might a referee stop the match?

There are a number of reasons why a referee might stop the match and why the ball goes out of play. Some of these are:

- If the equipment is faulty:
  - If a crossbar breaks, play must be stopped. Play cannot be resumed until the crossbar is repaired or replaced. If it can't be repaired or replaced, the match must be abandoned.
  - If the ball bursts, doesn't have sufficient pressure or is faulty, the match is stopped. The only person who can stop the match to change a ball is the referee.
- If a substitute comes onto the pitch without the referee being informed, the game will be stopped while the referee cautions the substitute and sends the player from the pitch.
- If a player is seriously injured and needs to be taken from the pitch, the referee will stop play until the injured player is removed from the field of play.
- If a player needs to be cautioned for a foul or misconduct.

How is the ball returned to play?

It depends on why the ball went out of play. If the ball goes out of play because it has crossed the goal lines or touchlines, a goal kick or throw-in will respectively be awarded. If a player has been fouled and the ball kicked from the field of play, in order for the injured play to receive medical attention,or respectively a free-kick may be given. Find out about throw-ins and free-kicks in Chapter 9.

More about substitution

Chapter 4 explains that, during a game, other squad members can be substituted for players already on the pitch. The rules of the competition explain clearly how many substitutes are allowed during a game. These rules were written to regulate the tactical substitution of players.

There is a straightforward routine for making a substitution that can often be seen during football matches. Players who come onto the pitch without following the regulations are cautioned by the referee and sent back, off the pitch.

The procedure for making a substitution is:

- The assistant referee is told that a substitution is requested. The substitute has to be one of the players nominated for substitution before kick-off.
- The assistant referee signals to the referee that a substitution has been requested (as shown above).
- A notice or board is held up showing the number of the player who is to come off the pitch during the next period of stoppage.
- The substitute then has to wait until there is a stoppage in the match.
- The player who is being substituted leaves the pitch first.
- Only when the player has left the pitch and the substitute has received a signal from the referee, is he or she allowed on the pitch. The substitute must enter the pitch by the halfway line.
- As soon as the original player leaves the pitch, he ceases to be a player and cannot come back into the game.

Scoring goals

- A goal is scored when the whole of the ball passes over the goal line, between the goalposts and under the crossbar, provided that the team scoring the goal hasn't broken any laws. If players have broken the rules or committed a foul and this has led to the goal, the goal may be disallowed.
- The team that scores the greater number of goals during a match is the winner.
- After a team scores a goal, the kick-off is taken by the other team, back in the centre circle. Each team has to be in their own half of the pitch
- A goal cannot be scored from an indirect free-kick or directly from a throw-in.

What if both teams score an equal number of goals?

If both teams score an equal number of goals, or if no goals are scored, the match is a **draw**.

But don't some games need an outright winner?

Yes, some competition rules and final rounds of tournaments require there to be a winning team at the end of 90 minutes.

How is a winning team decided when the match ends in a draw?

There are three possible ways of concluding a football match so that one team wins. They include the away goals rule, extra time and a penalty shootout.

1 The away goals rule

This is used as a way of breaking ties (draws) in matches contested over two legs. This means that two matches have been played. Each team has played at home once and each team has also played 'away', at their opponent's home ground.

The winner is worked out by taking the **aggregate score**. This means that the scores of both games are added together. If the aggregate score is tied, then the away goals rule is applied.

The team that has scored more goals away from home is declared the winner.

What if both teams have scored the same number of away goals?

If both teams have scored the same number of away goals, the second match will continue to be played into extra time. If the score is still level after extra time, a penalty shootout decides which team wins.

2 Extra time

Extra time is played after the 90 minutes of the match and all the stoppage time has been played and there is no clear winner of the match.

Is extra time always played like this?

Unfortunately, extra time is not always a question of just playing and attempting to score goals. The rules of the game allow for competitions and tournaments to make some changes. Extra time has produced some complicated formulae over the years called 'golden goals' and 'silver goals'.

What if the scores are still level at the end of extra time?

If scores are still level, there will be a penalty shootout.

3 Penalty shootouts

This method of deciding an outright winner is the most tension-filled method of arriving at a final result!

- In a penalty shootout, each team alternately takes five kicks from the penalty mark. It is very important that players stand in the correct place and that the five penalty takers are named, and take their kick in the order that the manager, coach and/or captain thinks best. Managers and coaches think very carefully about which players should have the responsibility of trying to convert a penalty kick into a goal.

- Team officials must leave the pitch before the penalty kicks can begin.
- If both sides have converted the same number of penalties into goals, kicks continue to be taken in the same order as before until one team has scored one goal more than the other from the same number of kicks. This is called **sudden death**.
- If a result is not arrived at during the first five kicks, other players from the team who were on the field at the end of the match must take a turn. Only when each team has taken 11 kicks and there is still no final result, can the players take a second penalty kick.
- Sometimes, it is clear before all five kicks have been taken who the winner is going to be. If a team has missed all three of their first penalties but the other team has scored three penalty goals, the team that winner. If this is the case, there is no need has already scored three goals will be theto finish taking the remaining penalty kicks – even if the other team did manage to go on to score two goals from their final two penalties, they have lost.

Which goal is used for a penalty shootout?

The referee decides this, taking into consideration factors that include the state of the pitch.

Who decides which team takes the first kick?

The referee tosses a coin. The captain of the team who wins the toss decides whether they want to take the first or second kick.

Can substitutions be made for the penalty shootout?

Only players on the pitch at the end of the match, including extra time, can take kicks from the penalty spot. The only exception to this rule is if a goalkeeper is injured during the penalty shootout, in which case he may be replaced by a named substitute, assuming that the team hasn't used all their substitutions during the game itself.

A penalty shootout can be a tense time for all involved.

Is the referee involved with deciding who will take a penalty kick?

No. The referee ensures that the kicks are taken properly and notes down the player and their number to ensure that the same player doesn't have a second kick until the rest of the players have taken their turn.

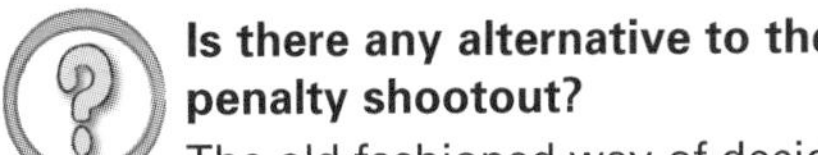

Is there any alternative to the penalty shootout?

The old fashioned way of deciding the winner was to draw lots or to toss a coin. This last method can sometimes still be seen in use where the referee decides that it is too dark for play to continue. This is something, however, that is unlikely to happen at the end of a big match!

Understanding the football results

Newspapers carry the football results. The teams are shown in their current position within their leagues.

P = games played

W = games won

D = games drawn

L = games lost

F = the number of goals that the team has scored

A = the number of goals scored against the team

GD = the difference between the goals each team has scored and the goals scored against them.

Pts (points) = teams are awarded three points for a win and one point for a draw.

Summary

1 Teams use different formations of players, depending upon whether they are playing an attacking or defensive game.

2 Strikers are players with a talent for finishing (scoring a goal).

3 The goalkeeper should organise the defence.

4 Defenders mark attacking players in the hope of closing them down. They also seek to challenge attacking players with the ball by tackling them.

5 Attackers seek to avoid defenders by using the space on the pitch to their best advantage. This may be achieved by using the blind side of the pitch or by making a cross.

6 Midfielders often have an overview of the game and move up and down the pitch in defence or attack, depending on how the game is going.

7 Players need to use a range of skills to kick, pass and dribble the ball.

8 There are different kinds of tackle but it is important to remember that the challenge should be aimed at the ball, not at the opposing player.

9 The referee decides whether a goal has been scored or not.

10 Matches that are played as part of competitions and tournaments often need an outright winner. If there is a draw in these circumstances, the winning team is decided using one or more of the following: the away goals rule, extra time or/and penalty shootouts.

11 The away goals rule calculates the winner according to the aggregate score and the number of away goals scored.

12 A penalty shootout requires each team to take a number of spot kicks from the penalty mark. Those kicks which do not go wide of the goal and which are not saved by the goalkeeper are converted into goals.

Training

A i Match the following players to the position they usually fulfil:

- Wayne Rooney
- Rio Ferdinand
- David Seaman.

ii Add to the list. Here are some to get started: Diego Maradona, Franz Beckenbauer, Zinedine Zidane, George Best, Rivaldo, Lev Yashin, Dino Zoff and David Beckham.

Goalkeeper	Sweeper	Defender	Midfielder	Forward

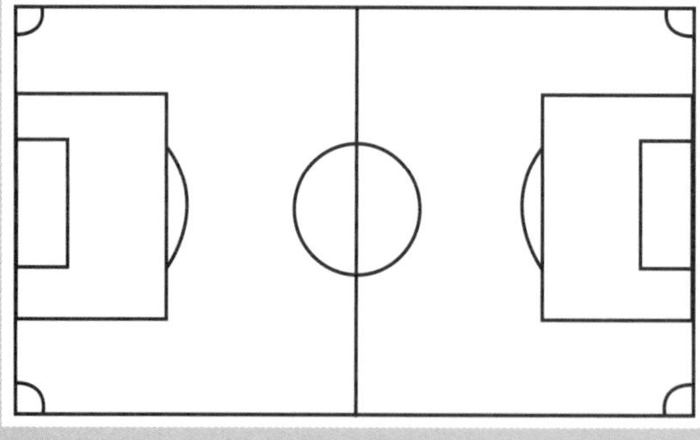

B i Watch an England match. Identify each player's name and position it on the pitch opposite. For instance, Steven Gerrard would be placed in the midfield.

ii Decide which formation the team has adopted.

iii Consider what the reasons might be for using this particular formation.

C Look at the diagram opposite. This shows the progress of the ball over the touchline.

A football follows the route ABCD. Decide whether the ball is in or out of play at the points indicated and note your answer in the boxes provided.

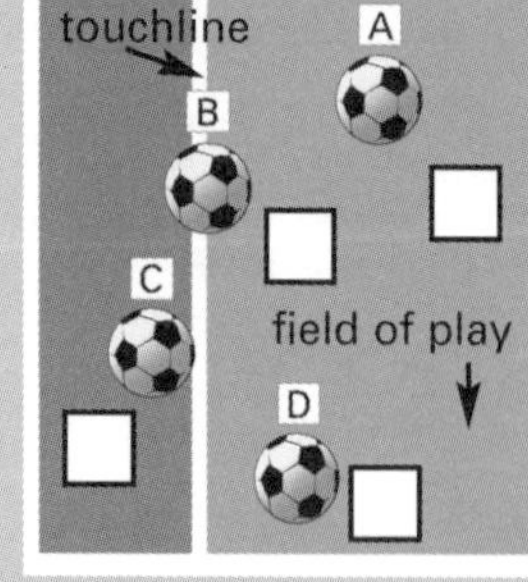

Chapter 7

The Offside Rule

Law 11 explains what it means to be offside and when this offence is committed. The rule, itself, is straightforward.

A player is in an offside position if he is closer to his opponents' goal line than both the ball and the second last opponent.

To remain onside, the attacker must have at least two members of the opposing team between himself and the opponents' goal line at the moment the ball is played to him. If the attacker is level with the second last defender or both of the defenders, he remains onside.

Law 11 goes on to explain that attacking players can't be offside if:

- the ball deflects off a defending player
- the player is in his/her own half of the pitch
- both the attacking and defending players are level with each other.

The complicated bit...

It is not an offence in itself to be in an offside position. The offence occurs and is penalised when the player is, in the referee's opinion, involved in active play.

If a player from the attacking team is standing on the edge of the penalty area, not involved in active play, he is not committing an offence. If the player is daydreaming, biting his nails, texting a friend or reading *Understanding Football*, he hasn't committed an offside offence. This is because he is not interfering with the ball. Therefore, he is not giving his team an unfair advantage, which he would have done if he was participating in active play.

You are involved in active play if you are:

- playing or touching the ball passed or touched by a teammate
- preventing an opponent from playing the ball by clearly obstructing the opponent's line of vision or movements, or making a gesture or movement that, in the opinion of the referee, deceives or distracts your opponent
- gaining an advantage by being in that position. Gaining an advantage means playing a ball that rebounds off a post, the crossbar or the referee, having been in an offside position or playing a ball that rebounds off an opponent having been in an offside position.

Now, remember the player who is reading *Understanding Football* while on the pitch. The player is offside but hasn't committed an offence, as he isn't involved in the game. The moment the player looks up, sees the ball heading towards him, sees the potential to score and then heads the ball into the net, an offside offence has occurred. If this player scored a goal, it would be disallowed. If the player failed to score and just interfered with play from a position that it is not permitted, a caution would be given. The other team would be able to take an indirect free-kick. A player also commits an offside offence if he impedes the play of a member of the opposing team.

Players who are concentrating on things other than the match, are guilty of unsporting behaviour. They may be shown the yellow card!

Remember, the player in the offside position has only committed an offence if the referee says he has. So, play to the whistle.

The referee's decision on the matter is final. However, arguments often arise when the game is analysed after the match because not everyone agrees with the referee's decision. Part of the problem is that the assistant referees often fail to see a player who is offside, or mistakenly indicate that a player is offside when, in fact, he isn't.

As the referee can't be everywhere at once, the assistant referees are there to help, ensuring the rules are abided by. However, when an assistant referee looks across the pitch, if the angle and line of sight isn't right, an attacker will appear to be offside when they are, in fact, onside. To be absolutely sure whether a player is offside, the assistant referee should be parallel to that player.

The referee also has to make quick decisions about offside because of the speed of the game, which also increases the chances of making an incorrect call of offside.

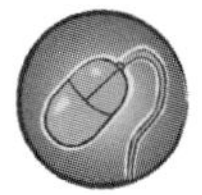

It's a proven fact! Check out the news story about the accuracy of assistant referees' offside calls at http://news.bbc.co.uk/1/hi/sci/tech/662691.stm

How does the referee know if the assistant referee has seen a player offside and if the player has either taken an active part in the game or impeded players from the opposing team?

The assistant referees signal what they see, to the referee, using a system of flags.

A referee's assistant signals that a player is offside.

Why is there an offside rule?

There's an offside rule to prevent a player from hanging around the goal ('goal hanging') on the off chance that a teammate would pass the ball to him to score a goal. If a player was allowed to do this, he would be perfectly set up to score a goal and the game would be very boring indeed!

Let me just check...if half a dozen players are waiting near the opposition goal area, with only the goalkeeper between them and the goal, they are all offside but haven't committed an offence?

Yes. Only when the players become involved or interfere with active play does any one or more of the players commit an offside offence. However, they're not being very sporting and will be warned by the referee.

If there are players not involved in the game in an offside position and another onside player scores a goal, does that goal stand?

Yes, as long as none of the offside players have interfered with the game.

Where does the offside rule originate?

The rule was created to stop 'goal hanging', as previously explained. It was first introduced in 1863 and stated that any player in front of the ball was offside. This was a bit of a problem when scoring goals and it was amended in 1868. From then until 1925, attackers had to make sure that they kept three players between themselves and the goal, in order to remain onside.

Finally, in 1925, the number of opposing players required between a player and the goal line was reduced from three to two. Apparently, this resulted in a much more exciting season and an increased number of goals were scored! In 2004, the rule was further amended so that assistant referees were required to wait to see whether players were actively interfering with play before identifying the player as committing an offence.

What is an offside trap?

An offside trap is a tactic used by the defending team. The defenders move forward, leaving the attacker behind them in an offside position.

Explore the offside rule further using this link, which illustrates its point with diagrams, at www.burtrandworld.co.uk/offside-rule.php

Do you think you've got the offside rule sorted? Test out your knowledge at www.news.bbc.co.uk/sport1/hi/football//4679881.stm

Summary

1 In order to be offside, a player has to have fewer than two of the opposition team (including the goalkeeper) between himself and the goal.

2 In order to be committing an offence, the offside player needs to be actively interfering with the progress of the game. To be involved in active play, the player must be playing with the ball or preventing an opposing team member from defending their goal.

3 Players cannot be offside if they:

- receive the ball directly from a goal-kick, throw-in or corner
- are in their own half of the pitch
- are level with a defender and there are two players (another defender and the goalkeeper) between them and the goal.

4 The assistant referees use a system of flags to communicate what they see to the referee.

5 The referee's decision is final.

Training

A i Look at the illustration below. When player B passes to player A, will an offside offence be committed?

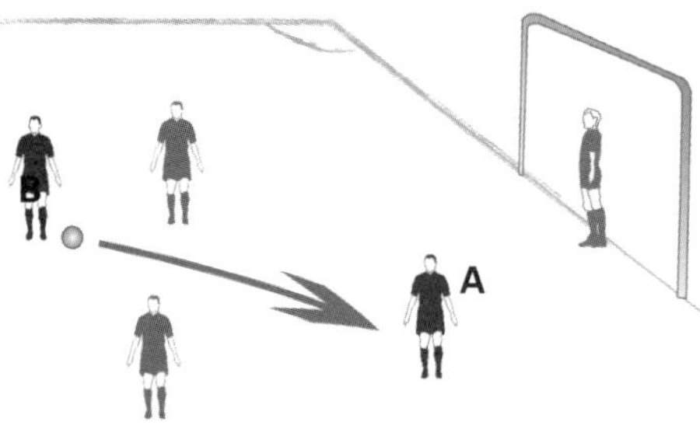

ii Explain how you came to this answer.

B Is the attacking player in the image (player B) offside? Explain your answer.

C Find a football match to go to or to watch on television. When it has finished, answer the following questions.

i How many offside players did you spot?

ii How many of the offside players went on to commit cautionable offences?

iii Can you explain each of the referee's decisions?

Chapter 8

Fouls, Misconduct and Booking Players

The aim of the football laws is to make the game as fair as possible for everyone. They ensure that both teams have an equal chance of winning the game. They also help prevent players challenging their opponents in a way that is likely to injure them. Football is a game for everyone. So, play fair and everyone will enjoy themselves.

The yellow and red cards

There are two ways of disciplining players on the pitch:

- Referees can caution a player (give them a yellow card).
  or
- Referees can send players off the field and out of the game (give them a red card).

Only a player, substitute or a substituted player can be shown a yellow or red card (it is possible to book a player who isn't actually on the pitch).

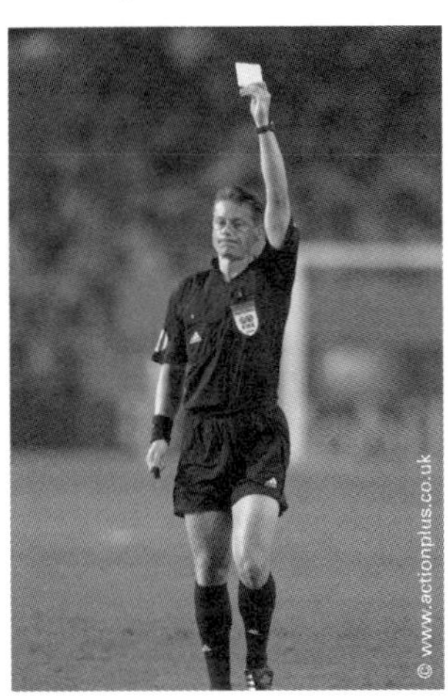

A referee holds up a yellow card.

Cautionable (booking) offences

Players are cautioned and shown the **yellow card** if they commit any of the following seven offences:

- Show unsporting behaviour.
- Disagree with the referee (either disagreeing with what he has said or what he has done).
- Repeatedly break the rules during the game.
- Waste time.
- Fail to respect the required distance when play is restarted with a corner kick or free-kick (the 10-yard rule).
- Come onto the pitch without the referee's permission.
- Deliberately leave the pitch without the referee's permission.

More about unsporting behaviour

Referees can find players guilty of unsporting behaviour in four different ways.

1 A player is guilty of unsporting behaviour if he does not take the game seriously. For example, a player who is reading *Understanding Football* or using a mobile phone during a game when he should be concentrating on the match, is guilty of unsporting behaviour.

2 A player is guilty of unsporting behaviour if he removes his jersey when celebrating a goal.

3 A player is guilty of unsporting behaviour if he breaks the spirit of the law while the ball is in play, or tries to get around the rules while taking a free-kick.

4 A player is guilty of unsporting behaviour if he deliberately deceives the referee.

Is a player cautioned as soon as an offence occurs?

Most of the time a player is cautioned immediately after committing the offence. However, the referee has a duty to ensure that the game flows smoothly because a stoppage can break player concentration as well as the momentum of a match. If a player comes onto the pitch without the referee's permission, the player concerned will be shown the yellow card when the ball is next out of play. The game won't necessarily be stopped at the exact moment the referee sees the player.

How is the match restarted after the referee has stopped a game to caution a player?

Play is usually restarted with an indirect free-kick given to the opposing team. The free-kick will be taken from the place where the ball was when the referee stopped the game.

Sending-off offences

Players are shown the **red card** and sent off if any one of these seven offences is committed:

- Serious foul play.
- Violent conduct (like hitting another player or a fan).
- Spitting at an opponent or any other person.
- Denying the opposing team a goal or an obvious goalscoring opportunity by deliberately handling the ball (this does not apply to a goalkeeper within their own penalty area).
- Denying an obvious goalscoring opportunity to an opponent who is moving towards the goal. The referee may also award a free-kick or a penalty kick.
- Using offensive or insulting or abusive language and/or gestures.
- Receiving a second yellow card in the same match.

A player who has been sent off must leave the vicinity of the field of play and the technical area (an area also known as 'the bench' where the substitutes, coaches and team managers watch the match).

Fouls and misconducts resulting in a free-kick or a penalty to the opposing team

If the referee believes that a player has committed any of the following 11 offences, in a **careless**, **reckless** or **excessively forceful way**, the opposing team will be awarded a **direct free-kick** from where the offence occurred.

This means that the player has deliberately used 'dangerous play' to challenge for, or play, the ball. Players can be booked for committing the following dangerous offences:

- Kicking or attempting to kick an opponent.
- Tripping or attempting to trip an opponent.
- Jumping towards an opponent.
- Charging towards an opponent.
- Striking or attempting to strike an opponent.
- Pushing an opponent.
- Tackling an opponent to gain possession of the ball.
- Making contact with the opponent before touching the ball.
- Holding an opponent.
- Spitting at an opponent.
- Handling the ball deliberately (except for the goalkeeper when he is within his own penalty area).

An **indirect free-kick** (taken from the place where the offence occurred) is also awarded to the opposing team if a player, in the opinion of the referee:

- plays in a dangerous manner (this isn't the same as 'dangerous play'. It means players have accidentally played in an unsafe way, possibly because they aren't aware of how close they are to their opponents)
- impedes the progress of opponents. This means the player gets in the way of a player from another team without intending to do anything useful for their own team and just stop the opposing player
- prevents the goalkeeper from releasing the ball from his hands.

These rules reflect the spirit of fair play, which is written into the laws of football and is given clear voice in the code of conduct. Players should treat other players in the way that they would wish to be treated.

The laws of football provide the referee with enough power to ensure that this fairness is maintained. On occasions, this might mean that the referee allows play to continue after a foul has been committed. This is called playing the advantage.

Playing the advantage

The referee uses discretion and experience to decide whether the game should be stopped when a foul is committed. If the referee feels that stopping the match will benefit the team that is guilty of the foul, he will let the game continue and will signal to play the advantage, as shown above. He will communicate this by shouting, 'Advantage. Play on', and sweeping both arms upwards and forwards in one strong motion. This shows that the ball should continue in play.

Is a direct free-kick or an indirect free-kick always awarded if a player commits a foul or is guilty of misconduct?

These fouls and examples of misconduct are punished when the referee feels that the player's behaviour is unacceptable. This can result in other players or someone watching the game believing that a foul or misconduct incident has been ignored by the referee. However, unless the referee thinks the behaviour is unacceptable, the ball will remain in play.

In addition, a penalty kick is awarded if a player inside his own penalty area commits any of the offences when the ball is in play, irrespective of the ball's position.

A tackle, which deliberately endangers the safety of an opponent, must be sanctioned as serious foul play. This behaviour is unsporting and dangerous.

What the rules say about the behaviour of goalkeepers

An indirect free-kick is awarded to the opposing team when a goalkeeper inside his own penalty area commits any of the following offences:

- The goalkeeper, who is controlling the ball with his hands, takes more than six seconds to release the ball.
- The goalkeeper touches the ball again with his hands after it has been released from his possession but has not yet touched any other player.
- The goalkeeper touches the ball with his hands after it has deliberately been kicked to him by one of his teammates.
- The goalkeeper touches the ball with his hands after receiving it directly from a throw-in taken by a teammate.

What happens if the goalkeeper saves the ball but then it rebounds off him? Isn't he parrying the ball, which is an offence?

The International FA Board (IFAB) states that 'the rules for the goalkeeper do not include the circumstances where, in the opinion of the referee, the ball rebounds accidentally from the goalkeeper, for example after he has made a save.'[1] So no, the goalkeeper hasn't committed an offence...unless the referee says so.

Booking players – the process

The referee sees a player committing a foul, or an assistant referee observes a foul and the referee agrees with this interpretation.

For example, Player A is tackling Player B by hacking at Player B's legs. This means that, rather than making a play for the ball, Player A is deliberately trying to bring Player B down.

The referee blows a whistle and raises either a yellow or a red card. This shows the player that an offence has been committed and what the degree of seriousness of the breach in the rules is. If the referee decides that Player A simply made a mistake when making a sliding tackle, Player A may receive a caution. If the referee decides that Player A has been unnecessarily violent, then the player may be sent from the pitch. The referee will make the final decision.

The referee writes the player's name and the nature of the offence in his notebook (this forms part of the referee's armoury).

If the player receives two yellow cards in one match, he is sent from the pitch.

After the match, the offending players are mentioned in the referee's report.

After the match, the continuation of the process depends on the tournament or competition that the match was a part of. If a player is sent from a pitch during a FIFA World Cup match, he would not be allowed to take part in the next game. Players in the English football leagues may be called before a disciplinary panel to decide whether they should be punished for their actions.

What if a referee doesn't see a player using a hand when he shouldn't, or if he deliberately pushes another player to the ground?

Unless the referee or one of the assistant referees sees an incident, there is nothing that can be done.

Can't players protest about unfair decisions?

The referee's decision is final. If the referee decides that a mistake has been made during the course of the match, he can, in theory, reverse a decision before the final whistle is blown.

Why are these rules imposed?

Football has moved on since medieval times, when matches resulted in murder and drove monarchs to make laws against the game. The key to the rules – both the letter and the spirit – is fair play. The referee helps maintain the letter and the spirit of the football laws.

[1]The FA (2006) 'Law 12 – Fouls and Misconduct', www.thefa.com/TheFA/RulesAndRegulations/FIFALawsOfTheGame/Postings/2002/05/12117.htm

Player profile

Gary Lineker was never booked during his entire footballing career, which he commenced as a football apprentice for Leicester City in 1977, before moving on to Everton. He began his England career in 1981 but didn't make his mark until the World Cup of 1986, where his six goals made him the tournament's top scorer. He has 48 goals on his national record, only one less than that of Bobby Charlton. He was voted Footballer of the Year on two occasions and, following his retirement from the football pitch, has become a familiar face on television.

Summary

1 When players are disciplined, they can either be cautioned with a yellow card or sent off the pitch with a red card.

2 There are seven cautionable offences: unsporting behaviour, disagreeing with the referee, repeatedly breaking the rules or making illegal moves, wasting time, failing to respect the required distance for a corner or free-kick, coming onto the pitch without the referee's permission or deliberately leaving the pitch without the referee's permission.

3 Players show unsporting behaviour when they are not playing the game to win, when they break the spirit of the law, when they set about deceiving the referee and when they remove their jersey to celebrate a goal.

4 Cautioning occurs at the time of the offence, unless the referee feels stopping play to caution the offender would interfere with the flow of the game.

5 The ball is put back in play with an indirect free-kick or a direct free-kick, depending on the nature of the offence.

6 The referee must decide whether a player is 'playing in a dangerous manner' (accidentally endangering the safety of players on the opposing team) or using 'dangerous play' (deliberately using unsporting tactics that threaten the safety of the opposing team).

7 There are seven sending-off offences. They are: serious foul play, violent conduct, spitting at someone, deliberately handling the ball to prevent the other team scoring, preventing a defender moving towards the goal by an offence punishable by a free-kick or a penalty, using offensive language or behaviour and receiving two yellow cards in one match.

8 Kicking, tripping, jumping on, charging at, striking, deliberately pushing, spitting at or holding onto an opponent or performing an illegal tackle, can result in a direct free-kick or a penalty being awarded to the opposing team.

9 If a player, other than the goalkeeper, handles the ball to prevent the opposing team from getting it, a direct free-kick or a penalty kick can be awarded to the opposing team.

10 An indirect free-kick is awarded if the player behaves in a dangerous manner, gets in the way of an opponent or prevents the goalkeeper from releasing the ball.

11 Indirect free-kicks are also awarded where goalkeepers, who are inside their own penalty area or fail to dispose of the ball within six seconds, touch the ball for a second time (when it has been released from their possession without another player touching it).

12 An indirect free-kick is also awarded if the goalkeeper directly receives the ball inside his or her own penalty area from a throw-in taken by a teammate.

13 Referees may continue a game rather than stop it to book a player, if a stoppage will benefit the team who has committed the foul. This is called playing the advantage.

14 Avoiding committing fouls and misconduct is not just about keeping to the letter of the law, they are also about keeping to the spirit of fair play.

15 Unless the referee or one of the assistant referees witnesses the foul, it cannot be penalised.

16 Players who are booked during the match are reported at the match's conclusion. They may go before a disciplinary hearing.

17 Know the rules and play by them.

18 The referee's decision is final.

Training

You are the referee. Choose from the following responses what you would do in each of the situations listed below (remember, you may want to choose more than one):

- Award an indirect free-kick
- Award a direct free-kick
- Award a penalty kick
- Show a yellow card
- Show a red card.

A A player enters the field of play without receiving a signal from the referee.

B As a goalkeeper releases the ball to kick it into play, an opponent intercepts it before it touches the ground.

C During a game, two players of the same team become involved in an argument that turns into an extremely nasty fight.

D A player tries to prevent the ball entering the goal by deliberately handling it. The ball, however, enters the goal.

E An attacking player is in an offside position and an assistant referee raises his flag. The referee does not see this but does see a defending player denying an opponent an obvious goalscoring opportunity in the penalty area. The referee stops play and then sees the signal of the assistant referee.

Chapter 9

Kicks and Throw-ins

This chapter outlines the types of kick that the referee can award to players, as a result of fouls or misconduct committed by members of the opposing team or as ways of restarting the game after a temporary stoppage.

There are two kinds of free-kick:

- Direct free-kicks

Direct free-kicks are awarded to the opposing team if a player commits a foul – this includes handling the ball. A goal can be scored from this kind of kick if the ball goes straight into the goal or if it is deflected off another player into the goal. In the unlikely event that a player kicks a direct free-kick into their team's own goal, a corner kick is awarded to the opposing team since, in the interests of fair play, it would not be fair to score the own goal.

- Indirect free-kicks

Indirect free-kicks are often awarded to the opposing team when players touch the ball illegally (excluding touching by hands). A goal can only be scored from this type of kick if a player other than the player who took the kick has touched the ball.

There are some rules that are common to both kinds of kicks:

- The ball must be stationary when the kick is taken.
- The kicker must not touch the ball a second time until it has been touched by another player.
- Players on the opposing team must be 10 yds (9.15 m) away from the player taking the kick.

Defending players taking free-kicks within the penalty area will take them differently from attacking players. There is more information about taking free-kicks in the penalty area later on.

Direct free-kicks

Direct free-kicks are used by the referee to compensate a team for a foul or misconduct committed by a member of the opposing team (see Chapter 8: Fouls, Misconduct and Booking Players).

A player takes a direct free-kick.

What does 'playing dangerously' really mean?

A player making a tackle with her foot raised, showing her studs so they are likely to injure the opposing player if they make contact, is playing dangerously. This is because of the reckless nature of the tackle.

A referee signals a direct free-kick

Is this still the case if the opposing player manages to avoid the dangerous tackle or action?

Yes. The referee may wish to play the advantage and talk to the player who committed the offence when play next stops.

The process

The referee raises one arm to shoulder height, pointing towards the direction where the kick should go. The other arm points down to the spot from which the kick should be taken.

The direct free-kick is taken from the place where the offence occurred.

The player taking the free-kick must be permitted to kick the ball without obstruction from the offending team. If a free-kick is taken outside the penalty area, all opponents must be at least 9.15 m (10 yds) from the ball until it is in play. If an opponent is closer to the ball than he should be, the kick is retaken. The player who stands too close to the ball before a free-kick is taken will be cautioned (shown a yellow card). If the player makes the same mistake a second time, the referee can give the player a red card (send them off the field).

The ball is in play when it is kicked and moved from the spot.

Other things to remember about direct free-kicks.

The kick will be retaken if the ball is not kicked directly into play, when a member of the defending team takes a free-kick from inside his own penalty area.

If, after the ball is in play, the kicker (who could be the goalkeeper) touches the ball a second time (except with his hands) before it has touched another player, an indirect free-kick is awarded to the opposing team. The kick is taken from the place where the infringement occurred.

If, after the ball is in play, the kicker (this still includes the goalkeeper) deliberately handles the ball before it has touched another player, a direct free-kick is awarded to the opposing team. The kick is taken from the place where the infringement occurred. If the infringement occurred inside the kicker's penalty area, a penalty kick is awarded.

Indirect free-kicks

An indirect free-kick is awarded to the opposing team if a goalkeeper commits an offence listed in Chapter 8 or an offence not mentioned in Law 12 that brings the game to a stop in order to show the player a yellow or a red card.

A player is 'playing in a dangerous manner' if she does not deliberately set out to but does commit a foul against the opposing player. It is an accident because the player doesn't know exactly where his opponent is and, therefore, endangers the safety of that opponent during the course of normal play.

The process

The referee blows his whistle before an indirect free-kick.

The referee signals that an indirect free-kick has been given by raising his arm above his head. The referee stays in this position until the kick has been taken and the ball has touched another player or goes out of play.

- A goal can only be scored from an indirect free-kick if another player touches the ball before it enters the goal.
- If an indirect free-kick is kicked directly into the opponents' goal, a goal kick is awarded.
- If an indirect free-kick is kicked directly into the team's own goal, a corner kick is awarded to the opposing team.

Direct and indirect free-kicks inside the penalty area

The image to the right illustrates a reference signalling an indirect free-kick. When a direct or indirect free-kick is awarded to the defending team:

- all opponents must be at least 9.15 m (10 yds) from the ball.
- all opponents must remain outside the penalty area until the ball is in play. The ball is only in play when it is kicked directly beyond the penalty area
- a free-kick awarded in the goal area is taken from any point inside that area.

When an indirect free-kick is awarded to the attacking team:

- it is taken from the point nearest to where the infringement occurred
- all opponents must be at least 9.15 m (10 yds) from the ball until it is in play, unless they are on their own goal line between the goalposts
- the ball is in play when it is kicked and it moves inside the goal area.

The penalty kick

Penalty kicks can be the most dramatic type of kick in the game of football, particularly if a match needs an outright winner. In a penalty shootout, players successfully converting a penalty kick into a goal can win the match for their team. A penalty is usually awarded during a match if the following things happen:

- If a defending player deliberately handballs inside the penalty area.
- If an attacking player is deemed, by the referee, to have been fouled inside the penalty area.

The threat of having a penalty kick awarded against a defending team aims to prevent the defending players from blocking the opposing team attempting to score a goal. If a player committed a foul near the goal line (for instance, a handball that prevented the ball crossing the goal line) and there was no such thing as a penalty kick, the team offended against would receive a free-kick. A free-kick is more easily blocked than a penalty kick, which would mean that the player who committed the foul would have effectively stopped the other team from scoring a goal. This is actually what happened in 1891 during a match between Stoke City and Notts County.

The penalty kick is a fairer way of compensating a team for fouls and misconduct committed against them inside the penalty area – a goal may be scored directly from a penalty kick.

If the kick isn't taken before the match reaches 90 minutes, the game will continue until the kick has been taken. This was written into the rules shortly after the penalty kick was first created as a result of a goalkeeper kicking the ball a considerable distance so that the game was over before the ball could be retrieved and the kick taken – an act that definitely had nothing to do with fair play! The image below illustrates a referee signalling for a penalty kick.

The process

Extra time is allowed for a penalty kick to be taken at the end of each half or at the end of periods of extra time.

The referee indicates that a penalty kick needs to be taken. The assistant referee may have signalled a penalty by raising the flag to chest height and holding it down, but this is not a FIFA-approved signal.

The ball is placed on the penalty spot. The player taking the penalty kick is properly identified. The defending goalkeeper remains on the goal line between the goalposts, facing the kicker, until the ball has been kicked.

The rest of the players must be on the pitch but outside the penalty area, behind the penalty spot. They must also be at least 9.15 m (10 yds) from the penalty spot.

When all the players are in the correct positions, the referee signals for the penalty kick to be taken. The referee decides when a penalty kick has been completed.

If the ball is touched as it moves forward, the kick must be retaken.

It is important for the kicker to stay calm and to not be distracted by anything. Goalkeepers often jump up and down and wave their arms in an attempt to distract the kicker. The penalty kick is a battle between the player taking the penalty and the goalkeeper. The kicker has to try to get the ball in the net while the goalkeeper is trying to put the kicker off (without breaking any of the rules) and to judge where the ball is going to go once it has been kicked. The player taking the penalty kicks the ball forward but must not play the ball a second time until it has touched another player.

If the kicker is sufficiently skilled and the ball travels with enough momentum, the ball will go into the back of the net. It doesn't matter if the ball deflects off the goalposts, crossbar or even the goalkeeper's body, as a goal has been scored!

A goal is awarded if the ball passes over the goal line in the usual way or if it rebounds in off the goalposts, the crossbar, the goalkeeper or any combination of the three.

If the ball rebounds onto the pitch from the goalkeeper, crossbar or the goalposts, play re-commences.

The referee and the assistant referees need to watch events carefully during a penalty kick. There is a fair chance that the kicker, the goalkeeper or one of the other players will break the rules before the ball is in play. The referee must make sure the kick is taken fairly and that the defending team defend justly, otherwise there are other sanctions that the referee can give out.

If the kicker breaks the rules before taking a penalty kick, the referee will allow the kick to continue, but if the ball enters the goal, the referee will not allow it as a goal and the kick will be retaken. If the ball does not enter the goal, the referee stops play and restarts the match with an indirect free-kick to the defending team.

If the goalkeeper breaks the rules, the referee will allow the kick to proceed and, if the kicker scores a goal, the referee will award it. However, if the ball does not go into the goal, the kick will have to be retaken.

If another player breaks the rules regarding a penalty kick, for instance a defending player gets too close to the penalty spot or moves in front of it, the referee will allow the kick to proceed. If the ball enters the goal, a goal is awarded. However, if the ball does not enter the goal, the kick is retaken.

If the player breaking the rules is an attacker and a goal is scored, the kick is retaken. If the ball doesn't enter the goal, the referee will give an indirect free-kick to the defending team.

How can attacking players break the rules of the penalty kick?

Attacking players can break the rules by entering the penalty area or by moving too close to the penalty spot.

What happens if the ball rebounds from the goalkeeper, the crossbar or the goalpost and is touched by a player who is in the wrong place?

If the ball rebounds in this way, the referee will stop play and restart the match with an indirect free-kick to the defending team.

What happens if the kicker touches the ball for a second time before it has been touched by another player?

If this happens, an indirect free-kick is awarded to the opposing team. The kick is taken from the place where the kicker touched the ball for the second time.

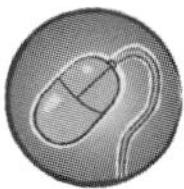

Find out about the history of the penalty kick by visiting www.fifa.ch/en/news/index/0,1464,22688,00.html?articleid=22688

Player profile

David Beckham was spotted by Tottenham Hotspur at an early age. After developing his skills at their football academy, he was signed by Manchester United when he was just 16. David's ability as a right winger combined with his phenomenal free-kick taking skills have turned him into an England legend and Real Madrid star. Since making his debut with the England team in 1996, he has gone from strength to strength, now as their captain. His dexterity, power and accuracy have made his free-kicks legendary – being able to 'bend it like Beckham' is every young player's dream.

The Throw-in

A throw-in is a method of restarting play if the ball has gone out by travelling all the way over the touchlines, thus completely leaving the field of play. A goal cannot be scored directly from a throw-in.

A referee signals a throw-in

An assistant referee signals a throw-in

The process

The referee may see the ball go out of play. The assistant referee might also signal that the ball is out of play if s he sees it travel over the boundary and then curve back in (remember, it's a split second movement).

The throw-in has to be taken from the point where the ball crossed the touchline. It can be thrown by any member of the team opposing the team of the last player to touch the ball before it went out of play.

Members of the opposing team must stand two metres or more away from the point at which the throw-in is taken.

At the moment of throwing the ball, the player taking the throw-in must face the pitch. She must have part of each foot either on the touchline or on the ground outside the touchline. Both feet must be on the ground. The player must use both hands to deliver the ball using an over-head throw.

The ball is in play immediately after it enters the field of play.

The thrower must not touch the ball again until it has been touched by another player.

Luke Young takes a throw-in.

Other things to remember about the throw-in

If the player who takes the throw-in touches the ball again after taking the throw, before it is touched by another player, an indirect free-kick is awarded to the other team.

If the thrower deliberately handles the ball before a second player touches it, a direct free-kick is awarded to the other team.

Taking a throw-in

- Grip the ball firmly but comfortably with both hands.
- Bring the ball back over your head.
- Your back should be arched to take the ball back further – your arms should be outstretched.
- Bring the ball forwards with your arms – this action is a bit like a catapult. The key is to generate rhythm and motion.
- Use the power of your back and shoulders to propel the ball forward as you release it and as it travels over the top of your head.

If an opposing player distracts or gets in the way of the player taking a throw-in, the opposing player is being **unsporting** and will be cautioned.

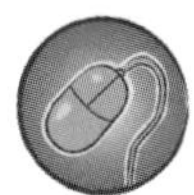

Find out more about the importance of taking a throw-in effectively, visit www.givemefootball.com/coaching/throwin.html

Do players ever kick the ball out of play deliberately?

Yes. Sometimes, if a player is injured, another player will kick the ball across the touchline to bring the game to a halt. It is really the referee's job to stop the game but this action by a player is seen as sporting. When the game is restarted, a player from the opposing team will take the throw-in. However, because the game was stopped because of injury, the ball will normally be directed back to the team who kicked the ball out of play. This is an example of fair play.

A goal kick

A goal kick is another method of restarting play. A goal can be scored directly from a goal kick against the opposing team. The referee will signal for this to take place as shown in the image.

The process

A goal kick is awarded when a ball, last touched by a player on the attacking team, passes over the goal line but a goal is not scored.

The referee signals for a goal kick by pointing towards the goal area.

The ball is kicked from any point within the six-yard box by a player on the defending team (usually the goalkeeper). The attacking team must stay outside the penalty area until the ball is in play.

The ball is in play when it is kicked directly beyond the penalty area.

The kicker is not allowed to touch the ball a second time until it has been touched by another player.

Other things to remember about goal kicks

If, after the ball is in play, the kicker touches the ball for a second time (except with his hands) before another player has touched the ball, an indirect free-kick is awarded to the opposing team.

If the ball is deliberately handled by the kicker before it has been touched by another player, a direct free-kick or a penalty kick (if the infringement took place in the penalty area) is awarded.

If the ball is not kicked directly into play beyond the penalty area, the kick must be retaken.

The corner kick

The corner kick was first introduced into football in 1872. It is another method of restarting play in favour of the attacking team and a goal can be scored directly from the kick.

A corner kick is awarded when the ball passes over the goal line, having been last touched by a defending player.

A referee signals for a corner kick to be taken.

An assistant referee signals for a corner kick to be taken.

The process

The referee sees the assistant referee signal that the ball has passed over the goal line but that no goal has been scored.

The ball is placed inside the corner arc at the nearest corner flag post. The ball can either be completely within the corner arc or it can be placed so that it overlaps the arc line. The flag post should not be moved. Members of the opposing team must stay at least 9.15 m (10 yds) away from the ball until it is in play.

A player from the attacking team kicks the ball. This player must not touch the ball again until another player has played it. If the player touches the ball again, an indirect free-kick is awarded to the opposing team. If the player handles the ball, a direct free-kick is awarded to the opposing team.

The ball is in play when it is kicked and travels out of the corner arc.

Other things to remember about corner kicks

- If the goalkeeper takes the corner kick, the same rules apply. However, if the goalkeeper breaks the rules about handling or touching the ball inside the penalty area, a kick is taken from inside the penalty area.
- For any other infringement, the kick is retaken.

Summary

1 There are 10 offences which will result in the opposing team being rewarded a direct free-kick.

2 It is possible to score a goal from a direct free-kick.

3 Before a goal can be scored from an indirect free-kick, a second player must touch the ball.

4 The opposing team must be 9.15 m (10 yds) away from the player taking the free-kick.

5 Free-kicks take place from the spot where the offence occurred.

6 Dangerous play is a deliberate act of recklessness that could endanger other players. Where a player is guilty of dangerous play, a direct free-kick is given to the opposing team. 'Playing in a dangerous manner' is a lesser offence and will be penalised by an indirect free-kick.

7 Penalty kicks are used to ensure there is a winner of the match. They are also used to penalise teams who commit offences inside their own penalty area that, if committed elsewhere on the pitch, would normally result in a direct free-kick.

8 The throw-in is a double-handed throw used to restart a game when the ball has gone out of play, over the touchlines.

9 A goal kick is used to restart the match when the ball has gone over the goal line having last been touched by an attacking player, but no goal has been scored. It is usually taken by the goalkeeper.

10 A corner kick is used to restart the match when the ball has gone out of play over the goal line having last been touched by a defending player, but no goal has been scored.

Training

A i Identify the 10 offences for which a direct free-kick will be awarded to the opposing team.

ii How far must defending players be from the kicker taking a direct or indirect free-kick?

B i Watch a football match. How do defending players protect the goal from a direct or an indirect free-kick?

ii Who is responsible for organising this sort of defence?

C i Watch a penalty shootout. Decide what skills the kicker needs in order to successfully score a goal.

ii What must a successful goalkeeper do in order to prevent penalty kicks being converted into goals?

D Look at the following pictures. Decide what is being shown in each of the images.

i

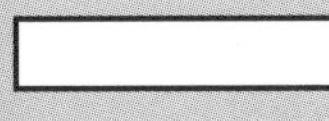

ii

iii

Chapter 10

Finding Out More

If you want to find out about getting more involved in football, why not join a team? You could join a school team or your local side. Get in touch with your local FA. They have a list of the grassroot teams in your area and will be able to help you find a club. Alternatively, you could join a soccer school to learn the skills you need to be a good player.

© www.actionplus.co.uk

To find out more about grassroot football teams, visit www.TheFA.com/Grassroots/GetInvolved/ and www.icfds.com

Glossary

Amateur A player who is not paid to play.

Angling A defending player moves position to reduce the area that offers potential to the attacking team.

Away A match played at a location other than a team's home ground.

Back of the net Every-day language referring to the area of the goal situated behind the goal line. The whole ball must cross the whole goal line for a goal to be scored.

Back-heel A backwards pass using the heel rather than the inside of the foot or the toe.

Bench The technical area where substitutes, coaches and managers sit near the pitch to watch the progress of a match.

Chip A stabbing pass, kicking the ball from beneath, usually resulting in the ball going over the opponent's head.

Clearance Moving the ball as far as possible away from the goal area.

Close down Mark an opponent to limit the opponent's opportunity of receiving the ball.

Create space Attackers avoid their marker to create an opportunity to receive the ball.

Derby A match between two local sides, for instance between Sheffield United and Sheffield Wednesday or Everton and Liverpool.

Dribble Move ball forward using footwork rather than passing to another player.

Far post The goalpost furthest away from the player with the ball.

Friendly A match that plays no part in a competition. It is played either just for the game's sake or for a special cause.

Gate The number of supporters attending a match.

Goal kick A kick taken by the goalkeeper when the attacking team has kicked the ball over the goal line but not scored a goal.

Hacking An illegal tackle involving a player attacking an opponent's legs rather than the ball.

Handball An infringement of the rules where a player deliberately handles the ball – the goalkeeper is not covered by this rule unless playing outside the goal area.

Home The ground where a team normally plays.

Injury time Another name for stoppage time.

Killing the ball A player controls a moving ball with their feet in order to make an accurate pass.

Late tackle A foul. A player tackles the player and not the ball. Whether accidental or not, this is still dangerous play and, at the very least, a caution may be given against the player.

League Football clubs playing against one another over the course of a season, with the top team winning the championship.

Linesman The former name for an assistant referee.

Mark To shadow the movements of an opponent to prevent them gaining the ball or to prevent them passing a ball freely.

Obstruction An offence in which a player hinders an opponent who is not in possession of the ball or makes a challenge by blocking the opponent.

Own goal A goal scored by a player against the player's own team.

Play-offs Matches played at the end of the season to decide which teams within a division will be promoted into the higher division or relegated (demoted) into the next division down. This means that divisions should contain clubs of a similar level of ability and skill, ensuring equality and interesting matches.

Promotion A team is transferred from one division into the one above them in the league at the end of the season, based on the number of points accumulated as a result of scoring goals during the season.

Relegation Clubs are demoted within a league from one division to the next one down at the end of the season, based on their performance and the resulting points accrued during the season.

Run An unbroken row of wins...or failures.

Save Successfully stopping the ball passing through the mouth of the goal.

Sell a dummy	Make an opponent believe the ball is going in one direction then send it in another direction.
Stoppage time	This is extra time added on to the end of the game to make up for stoppage time during the 90 minutes of the match.
Sweeper	A player who moves around the pitch as a defender where most needed.
Tackle	An attempt to remove the ball from an opponent. Poor tackles result in charges of dangerous play or playing dangerously.
10-yard rule	During a free-kick or a corner, all opponents must be 10 yards or more away from the player taking the kick.
Wall	A line of defending players who try to block shots at the goal during free-kicks. The goalkeeper usually organises the wall. The players must be 10 yards away from the player taking the kick.

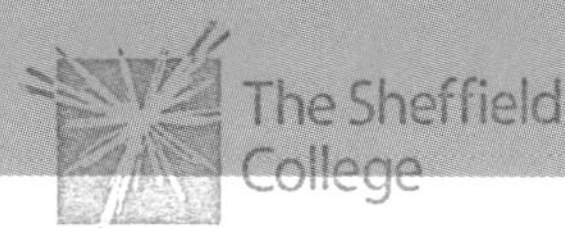

Answers

Chapter 5

A i and ii See diagram on page 13.

iii See table on page 12.

B Read pages 13–14.

C Read pages 17–18.

D • A coin to start the match.

• The yellow card and the red card for signalling what type of offences have been committed.

E The flag posts at each of the four corners of the pitch should have non-pointed tops, the game must be stopped if a goal is damaged and abandoned if it cannot be repaired or replaced. Players must not wear jewellery and they must wear protective shin pads.

Chapter 6

A Rooney: forward; Seaman: goalkeeper; Ferdinand: defender; Maradona: midfielder; Beckenbauer: sweeper; Zidane: midfielder; Best: forward; Rivaldo: midfielder; Yashin: goalkeeper; Zoff: goalkeeper; Beckham; midfielder.

C A, B and D are in play; C is out of play.

Chapter 7

A i Yes

ii Player A only has the goalkeeper between the ball and the goal. There needs to be two players between the attacker and the goal in order for Player A to be in a legal position. An offence has been committed because the player is actively involved in the game.

B No. The attacker is level with the second to last defending player not ahead of them. This means that the player is onside.

Chapter 8

A The player should be **shown a yellow card** for entering the field of play without the permission of the referee.

B It is an offence to prevent a goalkeeper releasing the ball from his hands. The releasing of the ball and the kicking are two parts of a single action. An **indirect free-kick** should be awarded.

C The referee should **send them off** and restart play with an **indirect free-kick** to the opposing team from the place where the offence occurred.

D The referee should award the goal and **show a red card to** the player for unsporting behaviour.

E This is a tricky one. If the referee accepts that the attacking player was offside, the defender is not sent off because no obvious goalscoring opportunity has then occurred. Play should be restarted with an **indirect free-kick** to the defending team. The player may be sanctioned, however, if in the opinion of the referee, the denying action on its own was a cautionable or sending-off offence. Alternatively, if the referee decides not to take on board the assistant referee's view of events, an offside offence has not occurred and the defending player should be **sent off** for denying an obvious goalscoring opportunity. Play is restarted with a **penalty kick** to the attacking team.

Chapter 9

A i see pages 43–44 ii 9.15m (10 yds)

B i They create a wall (a line of players between the kicker and the goal).

ii The goalkeeper.

D i Corner kick.

ii Penalty kick.

iii Throw-in.

Bibliography

Baddiel, Ivor (2002) 3rd edition. *Ultimate Football.* Dorling Kindersley: London. ISBN 140530550.

FIFA (2005) *Laws of the Game 2005.* This may be downloaded as a PDF booklet from http://www.thefa.com/TheFA/RulesAndRegulations/FIFALawsOfTheGame

Leith, Alex (1998). *Over the Moon Brian: The Language of Football.* Boxtree: London. ISBN 0752211684.

Lover, Stanley (1998) *Soccer Rules Explained.* Eric Dobby Publishing Ltd: Orpington, Kent. ISBN 1858820480.

Lover, Stanley (1999) *Football: The Game and Rules.* Chameleon: London. ISBN 1592286208.

Pickering, David (1994) *The Cassell Soccer Companion.* Cassell: London. ISBN 0304342319.

Useful websites

www.TheFA.com

www.SoccerBallWorld.com

www.scottishfa.co.uk

www.lcfds.com

www.socatots.com

Index

Figures in **bold** refer to illustrations.

Notes

Notes